The Counselor

A. W.

TOZER

The Counselor

MOODY PUBLISHERS

CHICAGO

Previously published by Christian Publications, Inc.
First Christian Publications edition 1993
First WingSpread Publishers edition 2009
First Moody Publishers edition 2015

The Counselor is an edited version of the Tozer classic formerly published under the titles *When He is Come* and *The Tozer Pulpit, Vol. 2.*

Interior design: Erik M. Peterson
Cover design: Faceout Studio
Cover photo of sunrise over lake copyright © by Corbis Photography/ Veer/CBP1055798. All rights reserved.

ISBN: 978-1-60066-796-1
LOC Catalog Card Number: 2009920548

We hope you enjoy this book from Moody Publishers. Our goal is to provide high-quality, thought-provoking books and products that connect truth to your real needs and challenges. For more information on other books and products written and produced from a biblical perspective, go to www.moodypublishers.com or write to:

Moody Publishers
820 N. LaSalle Boulevard
Chicago, IL 60610

1a 3 5 7 9 10 8 6 4 2

Printed in the United States of America

CONTENTS

———————•———————

CHAPTER 1

Whenever Jesus Christ Is Glorified, the Holy Spirit Comes

And when the day of Pentecost was fully come, they were all with one accord in one place. And suddenly there came a sound from heaven as of a rushing mighty wind, and it filled all the house where they were sitting. And there appeared unto them cloven tongues like as of fire, and it sat upon each of them. And they were all filled with the Holy Ghost, and began to speak with other tongues, as the Spirit gave them utterance. And there were dwelling at Jerusalem Jews, devout men, out of every nation under heaven. Now when this was noised abroad, the multitude came together, and were confounded, because that every man heard them speak in his own language.

ACTS 2:1–6

When we come to this important Scripture passage, the second chapter of Acts, I want us to consider something that is so often overlooked—the fact that whenever Jesus is glorified, the Holy Spirit comes!

Contrary to what most people unintentionally assume, the important thing here was not that the Spirit had come—the important thing was that Jesus had been exalted.

Now, let's summarize this chapter in Acts. Peter and all the disciples were gathered together when the day of Pentecost was fully come, and they were all with one accord in one place. Suddenly as they were gathered, "there came a sound from heaven as of a rushing mighty wind" (Acts 2:2). It was not a rushing, mighty wind—it was the sound of such a wind. It filled all the house where they were sitting. Little jets of fire sat upon each forehead, and they were all filled with the Holy Spirit, and they began to speak in languages. Seventeen nations were there and heard them speak in their own languages. The ones who could be amazed were amazed. The doubters doubted, and the questioners said, "What meaneth this?" (2:12).

Those who sat in the seat of the scornful were also present, and they said, "These men are full of new wine" (2:13).

"But Peter, standing up with the eleven, lifted up his voice, and said unto them, Ye men of Judaea, and all ye that dwell at Jerusalem, be this known unto you, and hearken to my words. . . . This is that which was spoken by the prophet Joel" (2:14, 16).

He proceeded to tell them how Jesus of Nazareth fulfilled prophecy and from there on, it was all about Jesus of Nazareth. In verses 32 and 33 Peter testified that "This Jesus hath God raised up, whereof we are all witnesses. Therefore being by the right hand of God exalted, and having received of the Father the promise of the Holy Ghost, he hath shed forth this, which ye now see and hear." Then in verse 36, "Therefore let all the house of Israel know assuredly, that God hath made that same Jesus, whom ye have crucified, both Lord and Christ."

So, the important thing, according to Peter, was the fact that Jesus had been exalted.

Jesus Himself had said on that last great day of the feast at Jerusalem, recorded in John 7,

> "He that believeth on me, as the scripture hath said, out of his belly shall flow rivers of living water." (But this spake he of the Spirit, which they that believe on him should receive: for the Holy Ghost was not yet given; because that Jesus was not yet glorified) (John 7:38–39).

It is plain that the glorification of Jesus brought the Holy Spirit, and we ought to be able to get hold of that thought instantly. So, we repeat: Where Jesus is glorified, the Holy Spirit comes. He does not have to be begged— the Holy Spirit comes when the Savior is glorified. When Christ is truly honored, the Spirit comes.

FAITH IN FAITH VS. FAITH IN GOD

Now, I want you to notice particularly Acts 2:14, "Peter, standing up with the eleven, lifted up his voice . . ."

He stood up, and then he lifted up his voice.

I would remind you that Peter here stands for the whole Church of God. Peter was the first man to get on his feet after the Holy Spirit had come to the Church. Peter had believed the Lord's word and he had received confirmation in his own heart. The difference between faith as it is found in the New Testament and faith as it is found now is that faith in the New Testament actually produced something—there was a confirmation of it. Faith now is a beginning and an end. We have faith in faith—but nothing happens. They had faith in a risen Christ and something did happen.

That's the difference.

Now, here was Peter, standing up, and he lifted up—and that should be the business of the Church—to stand up and lift up. Peter became a witness on earth, as the church should be, to things in heaven. The Church must be a witness to powers beyond the earthly and the human; and because I know this, it is a source of great grief to me that the Church is trying to run on its human powers.

Peter testified to something beyond the human and the earthly. Some power that lay beyond the earthly scene was interested in us and was willing to enter and become known to us. That power turns out to be none other than the Spirit of God Himself.

So, Peter, witnessing to things he had experienced, wanted to influence, urge and exhort those who had not yet experienced to enter in.

Now, a plain word here about the Christian Church trying to carry on in its own power: That kind of Christianity makes God sick, for it is trying to run a heavenly institution after an earthly manner.

For myself, if I couldn't have the divine power of God, I would quit the whole business. The church that wants God's power will have something to offer besides social clubs, knitting societies, the Boy Scout troops and all of the other side issues.

WHAT WE MUST DO

If any church is to be a church of Christ, the living, organic member of that redeemed Body of which Christ is the Head, then its teachers and its members must strive earnestly and sacrificially with constant prayer to do a number of things.

Fight Encroachment

First, we must strive to make our beliefs and practices New Testament in their content. We must teach and believe New Testament truths, with nothing dragged in from the outside. It means we must be going constantly back to the grass roots.

The men who pioneered our great North American continent took over a wilderness and conquered it. They went out with their axes, cutting down trees, building houses and then planting corn, potatoes, other vegetables and grain. You know, when they planted, they didn't go to bed and sleep until time for the harvest. They fought encroachment from the wilderness from the day they planted their corn and the rest of their crops until they harvested them and had them safely in their log barns.

The wilderness encroaches on the fruitful field, and unless there is constant fighting off of this encroachment, there will be little or no harvest.

I think it is exactly the same with the Church, for as one of the old saints said, "Never think for a minute that there will be a time when you will not be tempted. He is tempted the most effectively who thinks that he isn't being tempted at all."

Just when we think we are not being tempted, that is the time of danger, and so it is with the Church. We lean back on our own laurels and say, "That may be true of some churches, but it is not true of us. We are increased with goods and have need of nothing!" (see Revelation 3:17).

This is to remind us that we must fight for what we have. Our little field of God's planting must have the necessary weapons and plenty of watchmen out there to drive off the crows and all sorts of creatures, to say nothing of the little insects that destroy the crops. We have to keep after them. We must keep our field healthy, and there is only one way to do that, and that is to keep true to the Word of God. We must constantly go back to the grass roots and get the Word into the Church.

Seek the Power

In the second place, we must also earnestly, sacrificially and prayerfully strive to be empowered with that same power that came upon them.

Peter said, "He hath shed forth this, which ye now see and hear" (Acts 2:33). We must live to gear ourselves into things eternal and to live the life of heaven here upon the earth. We must put loyalty to Christ first at any cost. Anything less than that really isn't a Christian church. I would rather be a member of a group that meets in a little room on a side street than to be part of a great going activity that is not New Testament in its doctrine, in its spirit, in its living, in its holiness, in all of its texture and tenor. We need not expect to be popular in such a church, but certain fruits will follow if we make a church that kind of a church.

FRUITS OF A SPIRIT-FILLED CHURCH

Now, let's note some of the characteristics of a Spirit-filled and Spirit-led congregation.

Joy

First, they will be a joyful people.

The history of the Moravians tells how the Holy Spirit

came upon this movement one October morning in 1727. They were having communion. They went out joyful from that place, scarcely knowing whether they were on earth or had died and already gone to heaven. That joyfulness was characteristic of the Moravians for 100 years. They were not just a happy people in the sense of working up their happiness—their joy came from within.

We do have many professing Christians in our day who are not joyful, but they spend time trying to work it up. Now, brethren, I say that when we give God His place in the Church, when we recognize Christ as Lord high and lifted up, when we give the Holy Spirit His place, there will be joy that doesn't have to be worked up. It will be a joy that springs like a fountain. Jesus said that it should be a fountain, an artesian well, that springs up from within. That's one characteristic of a Spirit-filled congregation. They will be a joyful people, and it will be easy to distinguish them from the children of the world.

I wonder what the apostle Paul would say if he came down right now and looked us over in our congregations. What if he walked up and down the aisles of our churches, then went to the theater and looked them over, then on to a hockey game, on to the crowds at the shopping center and into the crowded streets? Then when he came back and looked us over again, I wonder if he would see very much difference. But where the Church is a spiritual Church, filled with the Spirit, we should always be able to distinguish the children of God from the children of the world.

Useful

Also, let us consider that a congregation that is Spirit-filled will be useful to the race of men.

I am not worried about what the critics say about preachers being parasites and the churches not producing anything, but I do believe that the Christian Church ought to be useful to the whole community. We can help the neighborhood where we live, and the neighborhood will be better because we are there as witnessing Christians. We don't need to apologize. Actually, they owe us a great debt, for our kind of transformed people keep the crime rate down, and where we have more God-filled, Spirit-filled churches we are going to have fewer policemen on the street. Wherever there's more godliness, there's less crime.

A Spirit-filled congregation is useful in the neighborhood—useful to the sons of men, even the ones that are not converted.

Influential

In another sense, we are to be influential among the churches, as well.

I would like to see a church become so godly, so Spirit-filled that it would have a spiritual influence on all of the churches in the entire area. Paul told some of his people, "ye were ensamples to all that believe" and "in every place your faith to God-ward is spread abroad" (1 Thessalonians 1:7, 8).

It is entirely right that I should hope this of you. I could hope that we might become so Spirit-filled, walking with God, learning to worship, living so clean and so separated that everybody would know it, and the other churches in our area would be blessed on account of it.

It is common knowledge that when Luther carried out his reformation, the Catholic Church was forced to clean up—the moral pressure from Lutheranism brought about change in the Roman Church. When Wesley came and preached throughout England, the Anglican Church was forced to clean up some of the things that were wrong. Methodism was a spiritual force that compelled others to do something about their own condition.

There is no reason why we could not be a people so filled with the Spirit, so joyfully singing His praises and living so clean in our business and home and school that the people and other churches would know it and recognize it.

The great thing about this is that when we have a Spirit-filled people who can live well, they can also die well. They began to look at the martyrs in the Roman days and said one to another, "Behold, these Christians die well!" Recall that old Balaam wanted to die the death of the righteous, but he wouldn't live the life of the righteous. We Christians ought to be able to die well—we should be able to do that if nothing else.

SOME WON'T LIKE IT

But, of course, there are some folks who just won't ever feel at home in a Spirit-filled congregation. Not all men have faith and there are some who don't want that kind of a church. I will name some of them now.

"Sunday" Christians

The people who put on religion as a well-pressed Sunday garment won't like that kind of a joyful church.

When we have a revival and the blessing of God comes to us and we do get the help we need from God, those who make religion merely a Sunday garment won't like it very well—in fact, they will be disturbed. From the biblical side, we will insist that they live right on Monday morning, and they don't want to do that. They want to keep their religion disengaged from practical living. Their religion is here and their living is over there. On Sunday they go in and polish their religion, but about 11 p.m. in the evening they put it on the shelf. On Monday they go out and live the way they want to live. I refuse to surrender to that kind of thing and to that kind of people. We are to be a church of the living God, and not a gathering of the influential and the big shots. The big shots can come if they get on their knees—a big shot on his knees isn't any taller than anyone else, you know.

Comfortable Christians

The people who refuse to let religion endanger them in any way won't like that kind of church and congregation.

They are those who refuse to let their church or their religion or their faith interfere with their pleasures or their own plans. They know about salvation, and they're willing to serve Jesus. They are on their way to heaven, they will make it through— but they are going to have fun on the way there, and they lay their lives out just as a gardener lays out the garden.

We lay out the plans for our own lives and say, "Now, Lord, it is nice to serve You and we love You, Lord, and let's sing a chorus," but we won't change our plans in any way.

But, let me remind you, the cross of Jesus Christ always changes men's plans. The cross of Christ is revolutionary, and if we are not ready to let it be revolutionary in us nor let it cost us anything or control us in any way, we are not going to like a church that takes the things of God seriously.

People want the benefits of the cross but yet they do not want to bow to the control of the cross. They want to take all the cross can offer but they don't want to be under the lordship of Jesus.

"Fun" Christians

The people who expect religion to be fun won't like that kind of a Spirit-filled congregation.

It is my belief that we have just gone through a long period when Christianity was the "funniest" thing on the continent. We have been told over and over that we could have more fun serving Jesus than we could doing anything else in the whole world. It is clean, too—and we don't have a hangover!

We have been taught in some good evangelical circles, "You serve Jesus and you can have all the fun you want, and you won't have that ugly hangover!"

That was Christianity for the sake of fun, Christianity as an entertaining medium. The whole thing is offensive and foul before God Almighty. My brother, the cross of Christ isn't fun, and it never was fun.

There is such a thing as the joy of the Lord which is the strength of His people (see Nehemiah 8:10); there is such a thing as having "joy unspeakable and full of glory" (1 Peter 1:8), but the idea that Christianity is another form of entertainment is perfectly ridiculous.

When I sing "Amazing grace, how sweet the sound," I am worshiping God Almighty. If you want to call "entertainment" that which they do before the throne when they cry day and night without ceasing, "Holy, holy, holy, Lord God Almighty" (Revelation 4:8), then I am an entertainer. If it isn't entertainment—and it isn't—then I am a worshiper.

The Church must worship, beloved! There is more healing joy in five minutes of worship than there is in five nights of revelry. Nobody ever worshiped God and went out and committed suicide as a hangover. Many a man has killed himself because he had just burned himself out trying to have fun. Many a pretty young woman has thrown herself into having fun, and before she is twenty-five she has to have a retread job done on her countenance—she has simply burned herself out.

Oh, how I love to see the grace of God in a face—don't you? I remember being asked to preach to a group of quiet, plainly dressed people, quite separated from the world in many ways and customs. The women had little black hats sitting on top of their heads and their hair was done up in buns. I had a tie on, you know, and I said to the man who was to introduce me, "You know, I'm a Gentile, and I don't know whether they will take me in or not."

He said, "Oh, preach to their hearts, and they will just forget that you don't belong to them." I did just that—and they did just that! I was just absolutely refreshed and wonderfully blessed.

Cultural Christians

Nor will the people who embrace a church for its cultural values be happy and satisfied in a Spirit-filled congregation.

Have you ever met these people? They don't know anything about the Spirit in their lives or the Spirit-filled church. They do believe the cultural value of the church is good for them and offers them something, and they want their children brought up in the cultural atmosphere of the church. They want book reviews and lectures on flower arrangements and child-rearing and all sorts of things—but it is a foregone conclusion that they are not going to be at home among God's dear regenerated people who are intent upon spiritual advance.

So, we will always have to be aware that this kind of discontent is going to rule out a few, and we are made sad by their decision. But we thank God for those who will be in their glory if we go constantly to the grass roots, weeding out everything that is not of God and keeping the grain growing lush and beautiful. Thank God for those who want to gear into things heavenly and walk with God and obey the truth and love each other!

WHO WILL THRIVE IN A SPIRIT-FILLED CHURCH?

Who are these people who will be happy and contented and fulfilled in a Spirit-filled congregation?

They Want to Be Rid of Their Sins

They are those who want to be rid of their sins. If I had a cancer growing on my neck I would want to be rid of it—the sooner the better. No one could come to me and say, "Now, I have a cowbell—let me shake it. Don't you like it?"

I would say, "No, I don't like it—I'm interested in this cancer on my neck. Do you have a cure for it?"

You say, "Aw, let's forget the cancer—let me jingle the bell."

Sometimes we have this kind in the church, but they are of no help. Let's talk about getting rid of our sins. Some people that are overwhelmed with the desire to be free from their sins have had refining fire go through their hearts sanctifying the whole. These people will be happy among us.

They Desire to Know God

The people who want to know God and to walk with God will be happy here, too. Their ambition is to walk with God and to "follow the Lamb whithersoever he goeth" (Revelation 14:4). The Lord's people know and appreciate one another. We may get an occasional bad apple—Jesus had Judas Iscariot in His little flock. We know each other and when we shake hands and someone says something to us about God, we sort of know we are talking to a brother in Christ. No matter what our backgrounds or where we came from—we all talk the same language if we are brothers and sisters in Jesus Christ, our Lord. We know and appreciate one another.

They Hear His Voice

Then, too, those who have learned to recognize the voice of the good Shepherd will be at home in a Spirit-filled church.

It is sad, to us, that some people have never heard the

voice of the Shepherd. His voice is as tender as a lullaby and as strong as the wind and as mighty as "the sound of many waters" (1:15). The people who have learned to hear and recognize the voice of Jesus—that healing, musical, solemn, beautiful voice of Jesus in His Church—are always at home where everything centers around Him.

The true Christian Church can be a conglomeration of everything under the sun. That is, we may have Calvinists and Arminians and Methodists and Baptists and all sorts of people, and yet we are all together on one thing— Jesus Christ is wisdom, righteousness, sanctification and redemption! He is All in all, and the people of the Lord who have learned to hear the voice of the Shepherd gravitate toward that kind of Church.

They Sense His Presence

Then, there are those who are sensitive to the Invisible Presence, and they will be at home in this group.

They may not be so sure about who else is present, but they know the Lord is present and they are sensitive to that.

Do you find your own heart sensitive to the Lord's presence, or are you among those who are "samplers" and "nibblers"? God help you if you are, for the child of the King isn't a sampler and a nibbler—he's a sheep who loves his Shepherd, and he stays close to his Shepherd. That's the only safe place for a sheep—at the Shepherd's side, because the devil doesn't fear sheep—he just fears the Shepherd. Your spiritual safety and well-being lies in being near to the Shepherd. Stay close to Jesus and all the wolves in the world cannot get a tooth in you.

There are those who have tasted of the good Word of God and felt the mysterious power of the world to come. Thank God for those in the churches who would rather hear the voice of Jesus than the voice of the greatest preacher or the best singer in the world. Thank God for those who would rather be conscious of the Divine Presence than be in the presence of the greatest man in the world. Thank God for those who are sick of their own sin and long to be holy—I pray that your numbers may increase. These are the things in which we believe: Jesus Christ the Lord; clean living, decency and separation from all things that are wrong; joyful, radiant, happy worship; sweet fellowship based on kindliness and patience, endurance and honesty. We believe in the missionary outlook, and above all things, "worship the LORD in the beauty of holiness" (1 Chronicles 16:29).

———————•———————

CHAPTER 2

The Holy Spirit Is Not Known through the Intellect

*John answered and said, A man can receive nothing,
except it be given him from heaven.*

JOHN 3:27

A s we consider this text, two things ought to remain in our minds. It states that we humans do not have the ability to apprehend divine things, but it also states that the ability can be given us from heaven.

It is quite plain in the scriptural revelation that spiritual things are hidden by a veil, and by nature a human does not have the ability to comprehend and get hold of them. He comes up against a blank wall. He takes doctrine and texts and proofs and creeds and theology, and lays them up like a wall—but he cannot find the gate! He stands in the darkness and all about him is intellectual knowledge of God—but not the true knowledge of God, for there is a difference between the intellectual knowledge of God and the Spirit-revealed knowledge.

It is possible to grow up in a church, learn the catechism and have everything done to us that they do to us, within reason. But after we have done all that, we may not know God at all, because God isn't known by those external things. We are blind and can't see, because the things of God no man knows but by the Spirit of God.

The Holy Spirit said through the apostle Paul, "even so the things of God knoweth no man, but the Spirit of God" (1 Corinthians 2:11). God knows Himself, and the Holy Spirit knows God because the Holy Spirit is God, and no man can know God except by the Holy Spirit. For any man to disregard this truth is to entirely shut out spiritual things from his understanding.

How I wish that all of our teachers in the church could understand that the realm of the Spirit is closed to the intellect. It is really not difficult to understand why this is so: The spirit is the agency by which we apprehend divine things, and the human spirit has died—it is dead because of sin. When I say that the human intellect is not the vehicle by which we apprehend divine things, I am not saying anything very profound. For instance, if there were a symphony being played just now, we wouldn't hear that symphony with our eyes, for God didn't give us our eyes to hear. He gave us our eyes to see.

If there were a beautiful sunset, we couldn't enjoy that

with our ears because God didn't give us our ears to hear sunsets. He gave us our ears to hear music, the voices of our friends, the laughter of children and birdsongs. He gave us our eyes to see those things which can be seen. He never confuses the two.

If a man stands up and says the realm of nature—visible nature—cannot be apprehended by the ear, no one gets excited. No one jumps up and says, "That man is a mystic!" He has only said that which is common sense, ordinary scientific fact.

When I say that God did not give us our intellect to apprehend Him, the Divine Being, but that He gave us another means of comprehension, there is nothing profound about that.

But at this point, let's share the Word of God in regard to this concept. Sometimes when we hear a thing explained and then we read the Scripture, it just comes alive for us.

We read in Isaiah 55:8–9,

> For my thoughts are not your thoughts, neither are your ways my ways, saith the Lord. For as the heavens are higher than the earth, so are my ways higher than your ways, and my thoughts than your thoughts.

Also, in First Corinthians 2:14 it says, "But the natural man receiveth not the things of the Spirit of God: for they are foolishness unto him: neither can he know them, because they are spiritually discerned."

The natural man—that is, the psychic man, the man of mind, the man of intellect—cannot understand nor receive the things of the Spirit of God. They are foolishness to him and he cannot know them because they are spiritually discerned. God gave us spirit to apprehend Himself, and intellect to apprehend theology—there is a difference.

In John 16:12–14, Jesus said,

> I have yet many things to say unto you, but ye cannot bear them now. Howbeit when he, the Spirit of truth, is come, he will guide you into all truth: for he shall not speak of himself; but whatsoever he shall hear, that shall he speak: and he will shew you things to come. He shall glorify me: for he shall receive of mine, and shall shew it unto you.

Now that is perfectly plain—the One who reveals God to us, who reveals Christ to us, is the Spirit of God.

In First Corinthians 2:6–9, we have a passage that tells us,

> Howbeit we speak wisdom among them that are perfect: yet not the wisdom of this world, nor of the princes of this world, that come to nought: But we speak the wisdom of God in a mystery, even the hidden wisdom, which God ordained before the

world unto our glory: Which none of the princes of this world knew: for had they known it, they would not have crucified the LORD of glory. But as it is written, Eye hath not seen, nor ear heard, neither have entered into the heart of man, the things which God hath prepared for them that love him.

It is strange how many times we stop when we should go on, and this is one of the places where people stop when they memorize, and put a full stop after those words "them that love him." We stop there but the Bible doesn't stop there. It has a little conjunctive "but" and it says, "But God hath revealed them unto us by his Spirit" (2:10). Eye has not seen nor ear heard nor the heart of man understood "but God hath revealed them unto us by his Spirit." Spiritual things are not apprehended by the eye, nor by the ear, and they are not apprehended even by the intellect. They are revealed by the Spirit, "for the Spirit searcheth all things, yea, the deep things of God" (2:10).

Paul uses an illustration in verse 11, saying, "For what man knoweth the things of a man, save the spirit of man which is in him?" Now that's what we call intuition, and that is not a word that we should be afraid of. With the help of God, I don't run from words. I am not afraid of the word "intuition" or "intuit," because that is how I know I am me—and not somebody else!

How do you know that you are you—and not some-body else? If you were to walk up to fourteen other men who looked exactly like you, it wouldn't stun you at all. You would smile and say, "Isn't this an amazing coincidence that fourteen other men look exactly like me." It could be that my wife wouldn't know the difference—but I wouldn't wonder which one I was. You maintain your individuality because of your intuition. You don't run to your old family Bible to find out who you are—you know who you are. If you were left an orphan you might not know who your parents were, but as far as your individual self is concerned, you know who you are by intuition. And you know that you are alive—you don't reason that you are alive. Now, let's apply this to the condition of the Church in our day. We forgot that there are some things that we cannot get hold of with our minds, so we run around trying to lay hold of them with our minds. The mind is good—God put it there. He gave us our heads, and it was not His intention that our heads would function just as a place to hang a hat. He gave us our heads, and He put brains in our heads, and that faculty we call the intellect has its own work to do. But that work is not the apprehending of divine things—that is of the Holy Spirit.

A FALSE CONCEPT THAT LEADS TO ERROR

Let me remind you now that modern orthodoxy has made a great blunder in the erroneous assumption that spiritual truths can be intellectually perceived. There have been far-reaching conditions resulting from this concept—and they are showing in our preaching, our praying, our singing, our activity and our thinking.

Error in Bible Study

I contend that we are in error to believe that Bible study can remove the veil that keeps us from spiritual perception.

I know that when we go to Bible school we have to learn theology, Old Testament and New Testament introduction, Old Testament and New Testament synthesis, and on and on it goes. The courses have long names, and I suppose the people who study them think they have something. They could have something, provided they have the divine illumination of the Holy Spirit. Until they receive that illumination—that inward enlightenment—they will not have anything because Bible study does not, of itself, lift the veil or penetrate it. The Word does not say "no man knows the things of God except the man who studies his Bible." It does say that no man knows the things of God except by the Holy Spirit. It is the Spirit who wrote the Bible and who must inspire the Bible. Let me quote a little motto—I don't recall where it came from: "To understand a Bible text takes an act of the Holy Spirit equal to the act that inspired the text in the first place." Personally, I believe that is true. In Second Timothy 3:16, Paul said, "All scripture is given by inspiration of God, and is profitable . . ." and that supports John 3:27, "A man can receiving nothing, except it be given him from heaven."

Error in Method

Now, I contend, also, that we are in a state of error when we believe that we can talk each other up and put spiritual things down on a level with man's understanding.

We say that a preacher is a salesman—he's out selling the gospel. But don't try to tell me that the methods God uses in winning men are the same as the brush salesman uses in selling a back scratcher. I don't believe it.

The Holy Spirit operates in another realm altogether, and the method of winning a man to God is a divine method and not a human one. Oh, we can make church members. We can get people over on our side, and they can join our class and go to our summer camps. We may have done nothing to them but make proselytes out of them. When the Holy Spirit works in a man, then God does the work, and what God does, according to the Scriptures, is forever.

We imagine that we can handle it by the flesh, and we do handle it by the flesh—the Lord lets us do it. We can hold the creed and not know God in His person at all. We can know the doctrine and not know spiritual things at all. The fearful consequence is that many people know about God but don't know God Himself. There is a vast difference between knowing about God and knowing God—a vast difference! I can know about your relative—and still not know him in person. If I have never met him, I do not know the touch of his hand or the look of his eye or the smile of his face or the sound of his voice.

I only know about him. You can show me his picture and describe him to me, but I still don't know him. I just know about the man.

A scientist knows bugs. He may write books on bees or worms or other bugs of various kinds and yet never know a bug—never! He could never get through to him!

If you have a dog, you can know all about him and his habits, but you will never really know him. He may smile at you, stick out his red tongue and pant. He seems to be intelligent, but he is a dog, and as a human, you have no facility, no organs, no techniques for getting into his dog world. You can comb him, wash him, feed him, trim his ears and you can know him externally, but you never can know your dog in this sense in which we are considering. Your dog can never know you. He can know about you, he can know when you are glad and when you are angry with him. He can know when he has done the right thing or the wrong thing.

Sometimes I think dogs have a conscience almost as good as people's, but still the dog dies and never knows the man, because he does not have the capacity given him to apprehend and perceive and understand as a human.

So it is that the human being can know about God, can know about Christ's dying for him, can even write songs and books, can be the head of religious organizations and hold important church offices—and still never have come to the vital, personal knowledge of God at all. Only by the Holy Spirit can he know God.

Again, it is my contention that as a consequence of this kind of error, we really have two Christs. We have the Christ of history, the Christ of the creeds. On the other hand, there is the Christ whom only the Spirit can reveal.

Now, you can never piece Jesus together out of historic knowledge—it is impossible. It is possible to read your New Testament and still never find the living Christ in it. You may be convinced that He is the Son of God and still never find Him as the living Person He is. Jesus Christ must be revealed by the Holy Spirit—no man knows the things of God but by the Holy Spirit.

I would like to make an emphasis here and make it clearly: A revelation of the Holy Spirit in one glorious flash of inward illumination would teach you more of Jesus than five years in a theological seminary—and I believe in the seminary! You can learn about Jesus in the seminary. You can learn a great deal about Him, and we ought to learn everything we can about Him. We ought to read everything we can read about Him, for reading about Him is legitimate and good—a part of Christianity. But the final flash that introduces your heart to Jesus must be by the illumination of the Holy Spirit Himself, or it isn't done at all.

I am convinced that we only know Jesus Christ as well as the Holy Spirit is pleased to reveal Him unto us, for He cannot be revealed in any other way. Even Paul said, "Now know we Christ no longer after the flesh" (author paraphrase of 2 Corinthians 5:16). The Church cannot know Christ except as the Spirit reveals Him.

EVIL CONSEQUENCES

There are several evil consequences of believing that we can know God with our minds, with our intellectual capacity.

First, the Christian life is conceded to be very much like a natural life—only jollier and cleaner and more fun!

The faith of our fathers has been identified with a number of questionable things. We must admit that one is philosophy, and I think that this modern neo-intellectual movement that is trying to resurrect the Church by means of learning is about as far off the track as it is possible to be, for you don't go to philosophy to find out about the Lord Jesus.

Now, the apostle Paul did happen to be one of the most intellectual men who ever lived. He has been called by some to be one of the six greatest intellects who ever lived, but this man Paul said to the church in Corinth, "And I, brethren, when I came to you, came not with excellency of speech or of wisdom . . . but in demonstration of the Spirit and of power" (1 Corinthians 2:1, 4).

If you have to be reasoned into Christianity, some wise fellow can reason you out of it! If you come to Christ by a flash of the Holy Spirit so that by intuition you know that you are God's child, you know it by the text but you also know it by the inner light, the inner illumination of the Spirit, and no one can ever reason you out of it.

When I was a young man, I read most of the books on atheism. I had my Bible and a hymnbook and a few other books, including Andrew Murray and Thomas à Kempis, and I got myself educated as well as I could by reading books. I read the philosophy of all of the great minds— and many of those men did not believe in God, and they didn't believe in Christ. I remember reading White's *Warfare of Science with Christianity,* and if any man can read that and still say he is saved, he isn't saved by his reading, he is saved by the Holy Spirit within him telling him that he is saved!

Actually, many of those philosophers and thinkers would take away all my "reasons" and reduce me to palpitating ignorance. On the basis of human reason, they would make a man just get down and walk out and toss his Bible on a shelf and say, "There goes another one!"

Do you know what I would do after I would read a chapter or two and find arguments that I could not possibly defeat? I would get down on my knees and with tears I would thank God with joy that no matter what the books said, "I know Thee, my Savior and my Lord!"

I didn't have it in my head—I had it in my heart. There is a great difference, you see. If we have it in our heads, then philosophy may be of some help to us; but if we have it in our hearts, there is not much that philosophy can do except stand aside reverently, hat in hand, and say, "Holy, holy, holy, Lord God Almighty" (Revelation 4:8).

Another of the questionable things is the manner in which we try to call upon science to prove Christianity.

We have just come through one of those long tunnels when the evangelical church was running to science to get some sort of help, not knowing that science has no technique for investigation of all that is divine in Christianity.

The things that science can investigate are not divine, and the things that are divine, science cannot investigate. Oh, science can make the satellites and the spaceships—many wonderful things in the human field—but all of that is really nothing. Christianity is a miracle and a wonder—something out of the heavens—something let down like Peter's sheet, not depending upon the world nor being a part of the world, but something from the throne of God like the waters of Ezekiel's vision.

Science knows nothing about that. It can only stand back, looking it over, and doesn't know what to say. But if we don't have this inner intuition, if we don't have this comprehension of the miraculous, we run to science. Some of those in this category say they want to believe in miracles. A fellow finds a fish washed up on shore and he gets a tape measure and crawls inside the bony skeleton and measures its gullet. He finds out that it is as broad as the shoulders of a man and he says, "See, Jonah could be swallowed by a great fish!"

Well, I believe the miracles—I believe them all, but I don't believe them because science permits me. I believe them because God wrote them and detailed them in the Bible. If they are there, I believe them!

You may have heard of the two scientists who reported that the story of Balaam's ass speaking to the prophet is false because "the larynx of a donkey could not possibly articulate human speech."

A thoughtful Scotchman overheard them and he walked up to them and said, "Man, you make a donkey and I'll make him talk."

There you have it, brother. If God can make a donkey, God can make him talk. Christianity stands or falls on Jesus Christ—stands or falls on the illumination of the Holy Spirit.

Peter could have reasoned until the cows came home and still not known anything for sure, but suddenly, when the Holy Spirit came upon him, he jumped up and said, "God hath made that same Jesus, whom ye have crucified, both Lord and Christ" (Acts 2:36). He knew that by the Spirit of God.

Still another of the questionable things is the manner in which we patronize human greatness when we have no inward illumination.

A system of literature has grown up around the notion that Christianity may be proven by the fact that great men believe in Christ. If we can just get the story of a politician who believes in Christ, we spread it all over our magazines, "Senator So-and-so believes in Christ." The implication is that if he believes in Christ, then Christ must be all right. When did Jesus Christ have to ride in on the coattail of a senator?

No, no, my brother! Jesus Christ stands alone, unique and supreme, self-validating, and the Holy Spirit declares Him to be God's eternal Son. Let all the presidents and all the kings and queens, the senators, and the lords and ladies of the world, along with the great athletes and great actors—let them kneel at His feet and cry, "Holy, holy, holy, Lord God Almighty!" (Revelation 4:8b).

Only the Holy Spirit can do this, my brethren. For that reason, I don't bow down to great men. I bow down to the Great Man, and if you have learned to worship the Son of Man, you won't worship other men.

You see, it is the Holy Spirit or darkness. The Holy Spirit is God's imperative of life. If your faith is to be New Testament faith, if Christ is to be the Christ of God rather than the Christ of intellect, then we must enter in beyond the veil. We have to push in past the veil until the illumination of the Holy Spirit fills our heart and we are learning at the feet of Jesus—not at the feet of men.

Now, consider with me the words of First John 2:27: "But the anointing which ye have received of him abideth in you, and ye need not that any man teach you: but as the same anointing teacheth you of all things, and is truth, and is no lie, and even as it hath taught you, ye shall abide in him."

What does that mean—"ye need not that any man teach you: but as the same anointing teacheth you of all things" (2:27)? The man who wrote that was a teacher, and we do not rule out the place of the teacher, for one of the gifts of the Spirit is teaching. What it says is that your knowledge of God is not taught to you from without. It is received by an inner anointing, and you don't get your witness from a man—you get your witness from an inner anointing.

Paul said, "For the preaching of the cross is to them that perish foolishness; but unto us which are saved it is the power of God. For it is written, I will destroy the wisdom of the wise, and will bring to nothing the understanding of the prudent" (1 Corinthians 1:18–19). And, "For after that in the wisdom of God the world by wisdom knew not God" (1:21). And, "Because the foolishness of God is wiser than men; and the weakness of God is stronger than men" (1:25).

Paul also assures us that:

But God hath chosen the foolish things of the world
to confound the wise; and God hath chosen the weak
things of the world to confound the things which
are mighty; And base things of the world, and things
which are despised, hath God chosen, yea, and things
which are not, to bring to nought things that are:
That no flesh should glory in his presence. (1:27–29)

You see, the Holy Spirit rules out and excludes all Adam's flesh, all human brightness, all that scintillating human personality, human ability and human efficiency. It makes Christianity depend upon a perpetual miracle. The man of God, the true Spirit-filled man of God, is a perpetual miracle. He is someone who is not understood by the people of the world at all. He is a stranger. He has come into the world by the wonder of the new birth and the illumination of the Spirit, and his life is completely different from the world.

If you want a scriptural basis for this thought, Paul said in First Corinthians 2:15, "But he that is spiritual judgeth all things, yet he himself is judged of no man." The spiritual man has a penetration that judges everything, but he himself cannot be judged by anyone, "For who hath known the mind of the Lord, that he may instruct him? But we have the mind of Christ" (2:16). That's simple.

Now, what are we doing to do with this truth? Are we going to argue about this? Are we just going to say that it was good? Are we going to do something about it? Are we going to open the door of our personality—fling it wide?

Oh, we don't have to be afraid—the Holy Spirit is an Illuminator. He is Light to the inner heart, and He will show us more of God in a moment than we can learn in a lifetime without Him. When He does come, all that we have learned and all that we do learn will have its proper place in our total personality and total creed and total thinking. We won't lose anything by what we have learned. He won't throw out what we have learned if it is truth—He will set it on fire, that's all. He will add fire to the altar.

The blessed Holy Spirit waits to be honored. He will honor Christ as we honor Christ. He waits— and if we will throw open our hearts to Him, a new sun will rise on us. I know this by personal experience. If there is anything that God has done through me, it dates back to that solemn, awful, wondrous hour when the Light that never was on land or sea, "the true Light, which lighteth every man that cometh into the world" (John 1:9), flashed in on my darkness. It was not my conversion—I had been converted, soundly converted. It was subsequent to conversion. How about you?

———————————•———————————

CHAPTER 3

The Presence and Ministry of the Holy Spirit: All That Jesus Would Be

*If ye love me, keep my commandments. And I will
pray the Father, and he shall give you another
Comforter, that he may abide with you for ever; Even
the Spirit of truth; whom the world cannot receive,
because it seeth him not, neither knoweth him: but
ye know him; for he dwelleth with you, and shall
be in you. . . . But the Comforter, which is the Holy
Ghost, whom the Father will send in my name, he
shall teach you all things, and bring all things to your
remembrance, whatsoever I have said unto you.*

JOHN 14:15-17, 26

I wonder how many Christian believers there really
are in the world today whose spiritual lives have been
transformed by acceptance of the fact that the Holy
Spirit has come as a Person and that He is willing—yes,

waiting—to do for us all that Jesus would do if He were here on earth?

I say this because I know what is happening in many churches in our land today. I say this because it is possible to run a church and all of its activity without the Holy Spirit. You can organize it, get a board together, call a pastor, form a choir, launch a Sunday school and a ladies' aid society. You get it all organized—and the organization part is not bad. I'm for it. But I'm warning about getting organized, getting a pastor and turning the crank—some people think that's all there is to it, you know.

The Holy Spirit can be absent and the pastor goes on turning the crank, and nobody finds it out for years and years. What a tragedy, my brethren, what a tragedy that this can happen in a Christian church! But it doesn't have to be that way! "He that hath an ear, let him hear what the Spirit saith unto the churches" (Revelation 3:22).

THE SPIRIT IS ESSENTIAL

The Spirit is faithful in His message that the restoration of the Spirit of God to His rightful place in the Church and in the life of the believer is by all means the most important thing that could possibly take place.

If you could increase the attendance of your church until there is no more room, if you could provide everything they have in churches that men want and love and value, and yet you didn't have the Holy Spirit, you might as well have nothing at all. For it is "Not by might, nor by power, but by my spirit, saith the LORD of hosts." (Zechariah 4:6). Not by the eloquence of a man, not by good music, not by good preaching, but it is by the Spirit that God works His mighty works.

Oh, that we could realize now the importance of throwing ourselves back on God and on the power of His Spirit, for there will be a day when we will have nothing but God. We had better act now while we can do something about it and bring the Holy Spirit of God back into the Church. Bring Him back by prayer, by obedience, by confession—until He takes over in our midst! Then there will be light, life, power, victory, joy and blessed fruit that will come to us. With His guidance and power we can live upon a different level altogether—a level that we never dreamed possible before. Yes, it is so!

Here let me remind you that the forces within Christianity have often committed blunders and then gone on to greater blunders.

In an earlier day, liberals within Christianity committed one of their great blunders in denying the deity of Jesus Christ and brought inner blindness to thousands, and spiritual decay and death to greater thousands.

Now, let's think about evangelical Christianity in more recent times. Many who attend our churches and others who have a part in leadership in our churches are committing a great blunder—they are neglecting the truth of the deity of the Holy Spirit. I do not believe truly evangelical Christians would deny the deity of the

Holy Spirit, but we have certainly neglected the truth of the place of the Holy Spirit's person in the Godhead, and of course, we have neglected His lordship within the Church.

THE RESULTS OF OUR FAILURE

In our own day, we must now confess that we can see many results of the failure of the Christian Church to honor the divine Person of the Holy Spirit.

"Social Club" Churches

First, the fellowship of the Church has degenerated into a social fellowship with a mild religious flavor.

In that regard, I want you to know where I stand—it is important and I want to say it plainly. I want the presence of God Himself, or I don't want anything at all to do with religion. You would never get me interested in the old maids' social club with a little bit of Christianity thrown in to give it respectability. I want all that God has, or I don't want any.

I want God Himself—or else I will go out and be something other than a Christian. I think the Lord had something like that in mind when He said, "I know thy works, that thou art neither cold nor hot: I would thou wert cold or hot. So then because thou art lukewarm, and neither cold nor hot, I will spue thee out of my mouth" (Revelation 3:15–16).

Unspiritual Teaching and Practices

Second, our failure to honor the Holy Spirit has allowed many unspiritual, non-spiritual and antispiritual teachers to be brought into the Church.

You know, the Church started out with a Bible, then it got a hymnbook, and for years that was it—a Bible and a hymnbook. The average church now certainly wouldn't be able to operate on just a hymnbook and the Bible. Now we have to have all kinds of truck. A lot of people couldn't serve God at all without at least a vanload of equipment to keep them happy.

Some of these attractions that we have to win people and keep them coming may be fine or they may be cheap. They may be elevated or they may be degrading. They may be artistic or they may be coarse—it all depends upon who is running the show! But the Holy Spirit is not the center of attraction, and the Lord is not the one who is in charge. We bring in all sorts of anti-scriptural and unscriptural claptrap to keep the people happy and keep them coming.

As I see it, the great woe is not the presence of these religious toys and trifles—but the fact that they have become a necessity, and the presence of the Eternal Spirit is not in our midst!

Now, if this is true, and we have any concern about it, we must ask ourselves if we really know who it is that we are ignoring when we refuse to give the Holy Spirit His rightful place of ministry in the Church and in our lives.

Here you are going to have to think, so shake your

head really hard and wake up some of the brain cells that haven't had a good workout since your high school or college days. I am asking you to think with me about something that is a little off the beaten track, keeping in mind that our main thought is the Holy Spirit.

ANOTHER MODE OF BEING

Consider with me, if you will, that "spirit" is another mode of being—spirit is not matter.

You can pick up a material thing and bounce it around, and that's matter. You are composed of matter—that head and that body are of matter, but that is only one mode of existence.

There's another mode, and that's spirit. The difference is that matter possesses weight and size and color and extension in space. It can be measured and weighed, and it has form. But the Holy Spirit is not material. Therefore, He does not have weight nor dimension nor shape nor extension in space. Now one power of spirit is to penetrate matter, to penetrate things of substance. Your spirit, for instance, dwells in your body somewhere, and it penetrates your body and doesn't hurt the body. It's in there penetrating because it's another form.

We know that when Jesus had risen from the dead He was no more mere matter. He came into a room where the door was shut and locked. He very evidently came through the wall somehow and managed to penetrate and get into the room without unlocking that door.

Now, He couldn't have done that before He died, but He did it afterward.

Spirit, then, is another kind of substance. It is different from material things, and it can penetrate personality. Your spirit can penetrate your personality. One personality can penetrate another personality. The Holy Spirit can penetrate your personality and your own spirit. In First Corinthians 2:11, the Bible says: "For what man knoweth the things of a man, save the spirit of man which is in him? even so the things of God knoweth no man, but the Spirit of God." It goes on to explain in verse 12 that no man knows the spirit things of God except the Spirit of God which reveals them. The Spirit of God can penetrate the spirit of man.

Confusion about the Spirit

I think you will agree with me when I say that many people are confused about the Spirit of God. The Holy Spirit, for instance, is not enthusiasm. Some people get enthusiasm, and they imagine it is the Holy Spirit. Some who can get all worked up over a song imagine that this is the Spirit, but this does not necessarily follow. Some of these same people go out and live just like the sinful world—but the Holy Spirit never enters a man and then lets him live just like the world that hates God. That is the reason most people don't want to be filled with the Holy Spirit—they want to live the way they want to live and to merely have the Holy Spirit as a bit of something extra.

I tell you that the Holy Spirit will not be just an addition. The Holy Spirit must be Lord, or He will not come at all.

Spell this out in capital letters: THE HOLY SPIRIT IS A PERSON. He is not enthusiasm. He is not courage. He is not energy. He is not the personification of all good qualities, like Jack Frost is the personification of cold weather. Actually, the Holy Spirit is not the personification of anything. He is a Person, the same as you are a person, but not material substance. He has individuality. He is one being and not another. He has will and intelligence. He has hearing. He has knowledge and sympathy and ability to love and see and think. He can hear, speak, desire, grieve and rejoice. He is a Person.

The Holy Spirit can communicate with you and can love you. He can be grieved when you resist and ignore Him. He can be quenched as any friend can be shut up if you turn on Him when He is in your home as a guest. Of course, He will be hushed into hurt silence if you wound Him, and we can wound the Holy Spirit.

WHO IS HE?

Now let us consider the question, "Who is the Holy Spirit?"

What Does the Church Say?

Well, the historic Christian Church said that the Holy Spirit is God.

Some of you could quote with me the Nicene Creed, which concludes: "And I believe in the Holy Ghost, the Lord and Giver of life who proceedeth from the Father and the Son, who with the Father and the Son together is worshiped and glorified . . ." That's what the creed said back there about 1,660 years ago.

Then there is the Athanasian Creed, and I thought it might be nice if I took you back about 1,200 or 1,400 years and we listened to our fathers tell who Jesus is. This came into being way back there when a man named Arius stood up and said that Jesus was a good man and a great man but He wasn't God. A man named Athanasius said, "No! The Bible teaches that Jesus is God." There was a great controversy, and some came to Athanasius and said, "The whole world is against you!"

"All right," Athanasius replied, "then I am against the whole world."

So they had that great gathering and there they pondered the matter. Out of it came the Athanasian Creed. You know, most of us are so busy reading religious fiction that we never get around to the creeds.

Here's what it says:

There is one person of the Father and another of the Son and another of the Holy Ghost, but the Godhead of the Father and the Son and the Holy Ghost is but one. The glory is equal and the majesty co-eternal such as the Father is, such is the Son, such is the Holy Ghost.

The Father is uncreated, the Son is uncreated, and the Holy Ghost is uncreated. The Father is infinite, the Son is infinite, and the Holy Ghost is infinite. The Father is eternal, the Son is eternal, the Holy Ghost is eternal, and yet there are not three eternals, but one eternal. So there are not three uncreated nor three infinite but one uncreated and one infinite.

So also the Father is almighty and the Son almighty and the Holy Spirit almighty. But there are not three almighties but one. The Father is God, the Son is God and the Holy Ghost is God, yet there are not three Gods but one God. The Father is Lord, the Son is Lord, the Holy Ghost is Lord, yet there are not three Lords, but one Lord. So the Father is God and the Son is God and so the Father is Lord and the Son is Lord and the Holy Ghost is also these things. The Father is made of none, neither created nor begotten, the Son is of the Father alone, not made nor created, and the Holy Ghost is of the Father and the Son, not made nor created nor begotten but proceeding.

Ah, brother, I don't know what that does to you, but that is just like a chicken dinner to my soul to hear and know that this had come down through the years, and that this is what our fathers believed.

Surely you know that in times past, when Christians met

and declared this kind of belief, some had their tongues pulled out, some had their ears burned off, some had their arms torn off, some lost their lives—all because they stood for this: Jesus was Lord, to the glory of God the Father.

These old saints of God were learned scholars who knew the truth, and they came there and wrote these things and gave it to us for the world and for the ages. On my knees I thank God for them!

What Do the Scriptures Say?

Not only does the historic Church say that the Holy Spirit is God, but the Scriptures declare that the Holy Spirit is God.

Here I should say this to you: If the church said it and the Scriptures did not say it, I would reject it. I wouldn't believe an archangel if he came to me with a wingspread of twelve feet, shining like an atomic bomb just at the moment of its explosion, if he couldn't give me chapter and verse. I want to know it is here in the Book. I am not a traditionalist, and when anyone comes to me and says, "It's a tradition," I say, "All right, that's very nice, interesting if true, but is it true? Give me verse and chapter." I want to know now: Were these old brethren right when they said all this about the Father and the Son and the Holy Spirit? Were they telling the truth?

Well, the Scriptures say He is God. They give to the Holy Spirit the attributes that belong to God the Father and the Son. Were they telling the truth? Listen to what the Scriptures have to say!

The Scriptures say He is God. They give to Him the attributes that belong to God the Father and the Son. In Psalm 139:7 it says, "Whither shall I go from thy spirit? or whither shall I flee from thy presence?" That is omnipresence, and not even the devil is omnipresent. Only God can claim omnipresence.

In Job 26:13, He is described as having power to create. It says, "By his spirit he hath garnished the heavens." Also in Job 33:4: "The spirit of God hath made me, and the breath of the Almighty hath given me life." There we have the breath, the guest, the ghost, the spirit of the Almighty giving life, so the Holy Spirit is here said to be Creator.

He issued commands—"the Holy Ghost saith" (Hebrews 3:7)—and only God can do that. He is called Lord in Second Corinthians 3:17: "Now the Lord is that Spirit . . ." and there is the baptismal formula, "I baptize you in the name of the Father and of the Son and of the Holy Ghost."

There is a benediction in Second Corinthians 13:14: "The grace of the Lord Jesus Christ, and the love of God, and the communion of the Holy Ghost, be with you all."

Yes, the Holy Spirit is God, and the most important thing is that the Holy Spirit is present now. There is unseen deity present. I cannot bring Him to you; I can only tell you that He is here. I can tell you that He is present in our midst, a knowing, feeling personality.

He knows how you are reacting to the truth of His being and personality and presence. He knows what you are thinking now. You cannot hide from Him—He is present now. Jesus said, "And I will pray the Father, and he shall give you another Comforter, that he may abide with you for ever" (John 14:16). So, He is here among us now. He is indivisible from the Father and the Son, and He is all God and exercises all the rights of God and He merits all worship and all love and all obedience. That's who the Holy Spirit is!

WHAT IS HE LIKE?

In this regard, there are some very beautiful things about the Holy Spirit that we should know and consider.

He Is Like Jesus

Being the Spirit of Jesus, the Holy Spirit will be found to be exactly like Jesus!

Some folks have actually been frightened by others making claims of being filled with the Spirit and then acting in every other way but like the Spirit.

Some who say they are filled with the Spirit are very stern and harsh and abusive. Others are found doing weird and unlawful things and they say, "That's the Holy Spirit."

My brother, the Holy Spirit is exactly like Jesus, just as Jesus is exactly like the Father. "He that hath seen me hath seen the Father" (14:9) Jesus said, and added, "Howbeit when he, the Spirit of truth, is come, he will guide you into all truth. . . . He shall glorify me: for he shall receive of mine, and shall shew it unto you" (16:13–14).

Jesus was saying, in essence, "The Spirit will demonstrate Me to you!"

I want to illustrate this truth a step further, answering some questions:

"What does the Holy Spirit think of babies?"

Well, Jesus thought of babies just like the Father does. The Father must think wonderfully well of babies, because the Son took a baby in His arms, put His hand on its little bald head, and said, "God bless you"—and He blessed the baby! Maybe theologians don't know why He did it, but I think I do. There is nothing softer and sweeter in all the world than the top of a little baldish baby's head, and Jesus put His hand on that little soft head and blessed it in the name of His Father. Now, the Holy Spirit is the Spirit of Jesus. The Spirit thinks of babies exactly as Jesus does.

So, we could ask, "What does the Spirit think of sick people?" I answer, "What did Jesus think of sick people?"

"What does the Spirit think of sinful people?" What did Jesus think of the woman who was taken in adultery and dragged into His presence? The Spirit feels exactly the way Jesus feels about everything, for He is the Spirit of Jesus. He responds exactly the way Jesus responds.

Think of Christ Jesus our Lord as being here in Person.

There wouldn't be anyone running away from Jesus. They came to Him. Mothers brought their babies; the sick, the wearied, the tired—they all came. Everyone came because He was the most magnetic Person who ever lived.

You will not find anyone saying very much against Jesus personally, because He was the most winsome, the most loving, the most kindly, the tenderest, the most beautiful character that ever lived in all the world. He was demonstrating the Spirit—and that's the way the Spirit is. When you think of the Holy Spirit, you will think of Him as gracious, loving, kind and gentle, just like our Lord Jesus Christ Himself.

He Can Be Grieved

Because He is loving and kind and friendly, the Holy Spirit may be grieved. We grieve Him by ignoring Him, by resisting Him, by doubting Him, by sinning against Him, by refusing to obey Him, by turning our backs on Him. He can be grieved because He is loving, and there must be love present before there can be grief.

Suppose you had a seventeen-year-old son who began to go bad. He rejected your counsel and wanted to take things into his own hands. Suppose that he joined up with a young stranger from another part of the city and they got into trouble.

You were called down to the police station. Your boy—and another boy whom you had never seen—sat there in handcuffs.

You know how you would feel about it. You would be sorry for the other boy—but you don't love him because you don't know him. With your own son, your grief would penetrate to your heart like a sword. Only love can grieve. If those two boys were sent off to prison, you might pity the boy you didn't know, but you would grieve over the boy you knew and loved. A mother can grieve because she loves. If you don't love, you can't grieve.

When the Scripture says, "And grieve not the holy Spirit of God" (Ephesians 4:30), it is telling us that He loves us so much that when we insult Him, He is grieved; when we ignore Him, He is grieved; when we resist Him, He is grieved; and when we doubt Him, He is grieved.

Thankfully, we can please Him by obeying and believing. When we please Him, He responds to us just like a pleased father or loving mother responds. He responds to us because He loves us.

This is the tragedy and the woe of the hour—we neglect the most important One who could possibly be in our midst—the Holy Spirit of God. Then, in order to make up for His absence, we have to do something to keep up our own spirits.

I remind you that there are churches so completely out of the hands of God that if the Holy Spirit withdrew from them, they wouldn't find it out for many months.

I said this once before in a message, and the next day a woman called me and said she had been visiting in our service.

"I belong to another church, and I heard you say that there are churches where the Holy Spirit could desert them, and they would never find it out," she said. Then she added, "I want you to know that this has happened in our church. We have rejected Him so consistently in our church that He is gone. He is no longer there!"

Her voice was tender, and there was no malice or criticism at all. I don't know whether she was right, for I doubt whether the Spirit of God ever leaves a church completely, but He can "go to sleep," so to speak, like the Savior who was asleep in the hinder part of the ship. He can be so neglected and ignored that He cannot make Himself known, and this can go on and on.

Let me assure you that this is the most important thing in the world—that this blessed Holy Spirit is waiting now and can be present with you this minute. Jesus, in His body, is at the right hand of God the Father Almighty, interceding for us. He will be there until He comes again.

But He said He would send another Comforter, the Holy Spirit—His Spirit.

We cannot be all that we ought to be for God if we do not believe and appropriate the fact that Jesus said, "The Comforter will be my representative, and He will be *all* that *I am*!"

CHAPTER 4

Pentecost: Perpetuation, Not Repetition

And when the day of Pentecost was fully come, they were all with one accord in one place. And suddenly there came a sound from heaven as of a rushing mighty wind, and it filled all the house where they were sitting. And there appeared unto them cloven tongues like as of fire, and it sat upon each of them. And they were all filled with the Holy Ghost, and began to speak with other tongues, as the Spirit gave them utterance. And there were dwelling at Jerusalem Jews, devout men, out of every nation under heaven. Now when this was noised abroad, the multitude came together, and were confounded, because that every man heard them speak in his own language. And they were all amazed and marvelled, saying one to another, Behold, are not all these which speak Galilaeans? And how hear we every man in our own tongue, wherein we were born?

ACTS 2:1–8

I want to discuss something based on the second chapter of Acts that is considered quite controversial—but I do not intend it to be controversial, but helpful.

I do not believe in a repetition of Pentecost, but I do believe in a perpetuation of Pentecost—and there is a vast difference between the two.

I want to try to discover with you the abiding elements of Pentecost as described in the book of Acts. What came and stayed? What came and went?

Now, as I said, I do not believe that Pentecost is to be repeated, but I do believe it is to be perpetuated. I believe that Pentecost did not come and go, but that Pentecost came and stayed.

You and I are living in the midst of it, if we only knew it.

It was true of Pentecost, as it is of all religious experience, that there were elements that were external—so they were variable. God doesn't care very much for the external. We ought to let the Holy Spirit teach us that God places little emphasis on the external aspects.

Then there are the elements which are internal and of the Spirit—they are permanent, and they are always about the same. Then there are elements which are incidental and so are of only relative importance—not that they are unimportant, but they are not critically important. Then, of course, there are elements that are fundamental and so are of vital importance.

We have read the historic facts in Acts 2. What did happen in that upper room in Jerusalem that day? There were about 120 persons sitting in that assembly when suddenly there was a sound in the room as of a rushing mighty wind. It does not say that a rushing wind went through, blowing everything. Did you ever hear a sound that gave you the impression that there was a great wind blowing somewhere? That is what it means—like the sound of a rushing mighty wind.

While they were wondering what it was, suddenly there appeared a great cloud of fire, and it divided up into little bits and sat upon the forehead of each one present. This fire was the divine Shekinah presence, and it divided up and sat upon the forehead of each of them.

It says, "tongues like as of fire." You light a candle, and you will see that the flame takes the shape of a tiny tongue—broad at the bottom and tapering up. That's all it means. This has no reference whatsoever to language. It says that the fire sat upon their foreheads.

Now, that's about all there was to it, except that they began to speak in other languages, and the people heard them speak in these languages.

UNREPEATABLE ASPECTS

Out of that historic occasion of Pentecost, what happened that can never be repeated? Let me give you some facts:

All the Church in One Place

First, there was the physical presence of all the Church together in one place. That was possible because there were only about 120 Christians. It could not be repeated after that because, on that day alone, there were 3,000 more persons born into the Body of Christ, and at another time there were about 5,000 who came to Christ at one time—that made about 8,000. I am sure they had no place in Jerusalem that would have seated or even housed 8,000 persons. As the gospel went forth from day to day, "the Lord added to the church daily such as should be saved" (2:47). Finally, the number of Christians became so large that no auditorium anywhere could have housed them.

The physical presence of all Christian believers together in one place was never repeated that I know of. That was one thing that happened at Pentecost that has never been repeated.

The Sound of Rushing Wind

As far as I can tell by church history and extensive reading, the sound of rushing wind from heaven was never repeated again, either. I have never read about that anywhere among the Moravians, Methodists, Presbyterians, Anglicans or any gathering of Christians other than this first group.

I have heard that when Dwight Moody called the Christians together, he took them out under the pine trees in the eastern part of the United States. He kept them out there several days and nothing happened.

Moody had to get up before them and say, "The meeting closes tomorrow, and we cannot go home without being filled with the Holy Spirit; let us go up again and wait on God." They went up among the pine trees, and the mighty Holy Spirit came down on them. The next day as they took the trains in all directions, the historian says that everywhere they went, they were like Samson's foxes going through the fields, setting fire as they went. The Holy Spirit had come, but He had not come with the sound of the wind. That was not repeated.

The Appearance of Fire

Neither have I read anywhere in Christian history that there was another appearance of a great body of fire. I am talking about the reliable and trustworthy accounts of reputable Christians who will not overstate their situations. I have not been able to find in any account that there has been the appearance of a great body of fire, dividing up and sitting on the foreheads of the believers.

Multiple Uninterpreted Tongues

I do not read that anywhere else or at any other time did every person in the group of believers begin to speak in a language that everyone else could understand without an interpreter. That is exactly what happened in Acts 2. I find no record of any other event or place where seventeen different language groups could hear the people speak and all of them know and understand what they were talking about without an interpreter.

I say that all of these elements of the day of Pentecost obviously were never repeated because in each instance they were external. The speaking in the languages was external, and the hearing and the understanding were all external. They were never repeated and never needed to be repeated.

Here is the logic of it. If these things were necessary to the Christian Church and necessary to the perpetuation of whatever took place at Pentecost, they would be considered basic and fundamental. If they were necessary to the Church's light and were never repeated, then the Church must have ceased to exist the day she was born, or at least ceased to exist at the death of those who were present.

Obviously, these external things were not the basic things. They were there and they were present, but they were external, they were incidental, they were elements that belonged to that particular historic scene.

PERMANENT ASPECTS

On the other hand, what happened there that day that did not pass away, that did not disappear with the sound of the wind, the sight of the fire on the forehead, and the seventeen languages being understood at one time?

What is the eternal and abiding element in Pentecost? Was something given, was there a deposit made? What came to pass that was internal, heavenly, permanent and lasting?

In order to discover what this element was, we must find out what was promised. According to John 14:16,

Jesus said, "And I will pray the Father, and he shall give you another Comforter."

In John 16:14, Jesus said, "He shall glorify me: for he shall receive of mine, and shall shew it unto you."

Christ Made Real

This was the promise: Someone was coming who would have the authority and the ability and the capacity to make Jesus Christ real to those who believed.

Remember what happened when the Holy Spirit came and fell upon those who were gathered: Peter leaped to his feet and said that these men were not drunk at all, but that something wonderful had happened to them, for "God hath made that same Jesus, whom ye have crucified, both Lord and Christ" (Acts 2:36). That which you now see and hear, Peter told them, this outpouring was shed forth by the Man at God's right hand, that is, the Lord Jesus Christ.

In John 16, Jesus had also said, "Nevertheless I tell you the truth. . . . I will send him unto you. And when he is come, he will reprove the world of sin" (vv. 7–8). The presence of the Holy Spirit is promised to show sinners their sin and to show Christ to the believers.

The "Ability to Do"

Jesus had said, "Tarry ye in the city of Jerusalem, until ye be endued with power from on high" (Luke 24:49b). A definition of the word "power" means the ability to do.

You know, because it is the Greek word from which our English word "dynamite" comes, some of the brethren try to make out that the Holy Spirit is dynamite, forgetting that they have the thing upside down. Dynamite was named after that Greek word, and the Holy Spirit and the power of God were not named after dynamite. Dynamite was discovered less than 200 years ago, but this Greek word from which we get our word "power" goes back to the time of Christ. It means "ability to do"—that is all, just "ability to do."

One man picks up a violin and he gets nothing out of it but squeaks and raucous sounds. That man doesn't have the ability to do. Another man picks up the violin and he is soon playing beautiful, rich melodies. One man steps into the prize ring and can't even lift his hands. The other fellow walks in and he has power to do, and soon the fellow who did not have the ability to do is sleeping peacefully on the floor.

It is the man with the ability to do who wins. It means the dynamic ability to be able to do what you are given to do. You will receive ability to do. It will come on you.

If you are a soul winner, you will have the ability to make the Word of God plain.

Whatever you do in the name of God, He gives you the ability to do. He gives you the ability to be victorious, to live right, to behold Jesus and to live with heaven in view. It is ability to do.

These are the vital and essential and eternal things that

took place at Pentecost and that came and stayed.

The wind, the fire and the appearance have never been repeated, as far as I know. But the Counselor came. He came and filled them. He came to abide in them. He came to make Jesus real. He came to give them inward moral ability to do right, and inward ability to do God's work. That stayed, and it is still here. If we do not have it, it is because we have been mistaught. We have been scared out of it. Some teacher has scared us out of it or some Christian has scared us away from the Holy Spirit.

SATANIC STRATEGY

This is a crude illustration, but let me tell you what we did after planting a field of corn when I was a young fellow in Pennsylvania. To save the field of corn from the crows, we would shoot an old crow and hang him by his heels in the middle of the field. This was supposed to scare off all of the crows for miles around. The crows would hold a conference and say, "Look, there is a field of corn but don't go near it. I saw a dead crow over there!"

That's the kind of conference that Satan calls, and that is exactly what he has done. He has taken some fanatical, weird, wild-eyed Christians who do things that they shouldn't, and he has stationed them in the middle of God's cornfield, and warns, "Now, don't you go near that doctrine about the Holy Spirit because if you do, you will act just like these wild-eyed fanatics."

Because there has been a lot of this weird stuff, God's

children are frightened, and as soon as you start to talk about it, they run for cover. They say, "Oh, no, none of that for me! I have seen dead crows out there in the middle of the field."

Well, my brother, I will not be frightened out of my rightful heritage. I will not be scared out of my birthright because some others didn't know what to do with the birthright or have found something else that has nothing to do with the birthright. I want all that God has for me!

Now, I want to point out something else here. When Christ was born many external things happened. They were not of ultimate or vital importance. When Christ was born the angels were notified and they came, but He would have been born whether they came or not.

When Christ came, He was born in a manger and there were all sorts of external circumstances, but there was one great vital fact that never has been taken back. He was born! He did come into the world. He became flesh and dwelt among us. He did come, and He took our human nature, and the Word was made flesh to redeem mankind on the cross.

That did take place, and it remains forever. The other external circumstances are not important. It is the internal things that matter. Thousands of people felt the saving power of Christ who had never seen the angels and thousands felt His healing touch who had never seen the wise men.

I take this, then, to be the eternal meaning of Acts 2

—that the Counselor has come! Deity is in our midst. God has given Himself to us, the liquescence of deity. Deity has been poured out. "Therefore being by the right hand of God exalted, and having received of the Father the promise of the Holy Ghost, he hath shed forth this, which ye now see and hear" (Acts 2:33).

WE NEED HIM MORE THAN EVER

I believe we are in a critical time in the life and history of the Church. If we continue to go the way we have been going in fundamentalist and evangelical circles, the fundamentalists will all be liberals and most of the liberals will be unitarian. We desperately need an outpouring of the Holy Spirit—and it cannot come as long as God's people refuse to acknowledge that we have failed to take advantage of our heritage.

God has promised us a unique afflatus, a seizure, an invasion from beyond us that is to come to us and to take over. It is to be in us what we can never be by ourselves. To write sonnets to compare with those Shakespeare produced, you would have to have the spirit of Shakespeare. The intellect of Shakespeare would have to enter your personality, because if you and I tried to write, "Shall I compare thee to a summer day," we would never get any further than that.

If you want to compose music like Johann Sebastian Bach, you would have to have the spirit of Bach. If you wanted to be a statesman like Gladstone, you would have to possess the spirit of Gladstone.

Now, if we are going to reproduce Christ on earth and be Christlike and show forth Christ, what are we going to need most?

We must have the Spirit of Christ!

If we are going to be the children of God, we must have the Spirit of the Father to breathe in our hearts and breathe through us. That is why we must have the Spirit of God. That is why the Church must have the Spirit of Christ.

The Church is called to live above her own ability. She is called to live on a plane so high that no human being can live like that in his own ability and power. The humblest Christian is called to live a miracle, a life that is a moral and spiritual life with such intensity and such purity that no human being can do it—only Jesus Christ can do it. He wants the Spirit of Christ to come to His people. This afflatus, this invasion from above affects us mentally, morally and spiritually.

HOW TO PREPARE FOR HIM

What about preparation for God's working among us by His Spirit?

I believe that it might be well for us if we just stopped all of our business and got quiet and worshiped God and waited on Him. It doesn't make me popular when I remind you that we are a carnal bunch, but it is true, nevertheless, that the body of Christians is carnal. The Lord's people ought to be a sanctified, pure, clean people, but we are a carnal crowd. We are carnal in our attitudes, in our tastes and carnal in many things. Our young people often are not reverent in our Christian services. We have so degraded our religious tastes that our Christian service is largely exhibitionism. We desperately need a divine visitation—for our situation will never be cured by sermons! It will never be cured until the Church of Christ has suddenly been confronted with what one man called the *mysterium tremendium*—the fearful mystery that is God, the fearful majesty that is God. This is what the Holy Spirit does. He brings the wonderful mystery that is God to us, and presents Him to the human spirit.

We are confronted with this and out goes our irreverence, out goes our carnality, out goes our degraded religious tastes, out goes all of these things, and the soul, held speechless, trembles inwardly to the fiber of its being. The Holy Spirit bestows upon us a beatitude beyond compare.

We will never know more about God than the Spirit teaches us. We will never know any more about Jesus than the Spirit teaches us, because there is only the Spirit to do the teaching. Oh, Holy Spirit, how we have grieved You! How we have insulted You! How we have rejected You!

He is our Teacher, and if He does not teach us, we never can know. He is our Illuminator, and if He does not turn on the light, we never can see. He is the Healer of our deaf ears, and if He does not touch our ears, we never can hear. Churches can run for weeks and months and years without knowing anything about this or having the Spirit of the living God fall upon them. Oh, my heart, be still before Him, prostrate, inwardly adore Him!

HE IS HERE AMONG US

This, then, is the news I have for you—Deity is present! Pentecost means that the Deity came to mankind to give Himself to man, that man might breathe Him in as he breathes in the air, that He might fill men. Dr. A. B. Simpson used an illustration which was about as good as any I ever heard. He said, "Being filled with the fullness of God is like a bottle in the ocean. You take the cork out of the bottle and sink it in the ocean, and you have the bottle completely full of ocean. The bottle is in the ocean, and the ocean is in the bottle. The ocean contains the bottle, but the bottle contains only a little bit of the ocean. So it is with a Christian."

We are filled unto the fullness of God, but, of course, we cannot contain all of God because God contains us; but we can have all of God that we can contain. If we only knew it, we could enlarge our vessel. The vessel gets bigger as we go on with God. Deity is among us. If a celebrity should visit our churches, the ushers would not know what to do with all of the people. I tell you we have a celebrity in our midst: "And suddenly there came. . . . And they were all filled with the Holy Ghost" (Acts 2:2, 4).

Deity came down among us, and He came to stay—not to come and go, but to come and stay!

Oh, the shame that we should ignore the presence of royalty. We have higher than earthly royalty—we have the Lord of lords and the King of kings—we have the blessed Holy Spirit present, and we are treating Him as if He were not present at all.

We resist Him, disobey Him, quench Him and compromise with our hearts. We hear a sermon about Him and determine to learn more and do something about it. Our conviction wears off, and soon we go back to the same old dead level we were in before. We resist the blessed Counselor. He has come to comfort. He has come to teach. He is the Spirit of instruction. He has come to bring light, for He is the Spirit of light. He comes to bring purity, for He is the Spirit of holiness. He comes to bring power, for He is the Spirit of power.

He comes to bring these blessings to our hearts, and He wants us to have this kind of experience. God will do this for people. He doesn't ask our denominational background. He doesn't ask whether we are Arminian or Calvinist. He asks nothing except that we be willing to obey, willing to listen, willing to stop disobeying.

Are you willing to stop quenching the Spirit? Are you willing to stop resisting the Spirit?

He only asks that you throw up your hands in surrender and say, "I believe Deity is present." Breathe in the Holy Spirit, and let Him come and fill your life.

That is it? Perhaps it does not sound as dramatic and colorful as you have been taught that things ought to be, but here we have it. The Holy Spirit came, and He is still here. All He wants is for us to yield, obey, open our hearts, and He rushes in and our lives are transformed and changed!

———————•———————

CHAPTER 5

The Promised Filling of the Holy Spirit: Instantly, Not Gradually

And we are his witnesses of these things; and so is also the Holy Ghost, whom God hath given to them that obey him.

ACTS 5:32

If ye then, being evil, know how to give good gifts unto your children: how much more shall your heavenly Father give the Holy Spirit to them that ask him?

LUKE 11:13

This only would I learn of you, Received ye the Spirit by the works of the law, or by the hearing of faith? Are ye so foolish? having begun in the Spirit, are ye now made perfect by the flesh?

GALATIANS 3:2–3

There are many people in our churches who would like to think that they are filled with the Holy Spirit—even though they don't know it. This is a most shocking thing, and I am sure that this is one of the attitudes through which Satan opposes the doctrine of the genuine Spirit-filled life. And yet, our people don't want to hear too much about it.

Let me say that I do not find in the Old Testament or in the New Testament, neither in Christian biography, in Church history or in personal Christian testimonies, the experience of any person who was ever filled with Holy Spirit and didn't know it!

I can be dogmatic about this on the basis of deep study: No one was ever filled with the Holy Spirit who didn't know that he had been so filled! Furthermore, none of the persons in the Bible and none that I can find in Church history or biography was ever filled with the Holy Spirit who didn't know when he was filled. I cannot find that anyone was ever filled gradually.

Now, as I said, Satan opposes the doctrine of the Spirit-filled life about as bitterly as any doctrine there is. He has confused it, opposed it, surrounded it with false notions and fears. The devil knows that if we will just say that we want to be filled gradually, he will have no more worries from us—because that process is so slow. You might encourage yourself: "Well, I am a little fuller today than I was yesterday," or at least, "I am a little fuller this year than I was last year."

This is a place for carnal creatures to hide. It is a place for carnal church members to hide. In the Scriptures, it was never a gradual filling. It says that He fell upon them, He came upon them, He filled them—it was an instantaneous act.

You may say, "Well, I am going to be filled gradually!"

I answer, my brother, that you are not. You are going to be filled as an act or you are not going to be filled—you can be sure of that!

We ought to be very plain in our teaching that Satan has blocked every effort of the Church of Christ to receive from the Father her divine and blood-bought patrimony that the Holy Spirit should fill His Church and that He should fill individuals who make up His Church.

If we really mean business about pressing on to follow the Lord, we will be brought to the conclusion that it was His plan, and part of the purchase of the blood of Christ, that He should fill everyone who names the name of Jesus. There isn't anything about the Spirit-filled life that is abnormal, extra, strange or queer. Actually, it is the way Christians are supposed to be!

SOME THINGS TO BE SETTLED

There are some matters that have to be settled in our own beings before we can move on to the question of how to be filled with the Spirit of God.

Are You Sure You Can Be Filled?

This is the first: Before you can be filled with the Spirit, you must be sure, to the point of conviction, that you can be filled.

If you have any doubt, if someone has dropped a doctrinal question in your mind and left the impression with you that you received everything God has for you the day you received Christ as your Savior, you will never move on to the fullness.

Now, at this point I believe in complete realism—salty, down-to-earth realism. Not everyone who listens to me is going to be filled with the Spirit. Some are going to be filled, for every once in awhile someone comes with a shining face and says, "Well, it happened! God has done it!" From that time on, that life is transformed. Spirit-filled Christians are changed people.

Unless you are convinced about this, I recommend that you don't do anything yet. I would rather have you meditate on the Scriptures, read the Word and see for yourselves what God the Lord has spoken.

Do You Really Want to Be Filled?

Then, this is the second matter to be settled: You must be sure that you desire to be filled.

Someone will say, "Doesn't everybody desire to be filled?" and the answer is "No." I suppose many people desire to be full but not many desire to be filled. I want to responsibly declare that before you can be filled with the Spirit, you must desire to be, and that some people do not desire to be filled.

Are you sure, for instance, that you are willing to be possessed by a spirit? You have heard of spiritpossession, I am sure, but there are two kinds of spirit-possession. There is the possession by evil spirits, where a human personality can be completely submerged, as in the days of Jesus, making it filthy or dumb or evil. Jesus cast out spirits such as these—but they were spirits, and they did possess human personality.

It is plain in the Scriptures that the gentle and good Holy Spirit wants to fill us and possess us if we are Christians. This Spirit is like Jesus. Do you want to be possessed by a Spirit that is like Jesus— a Spirit that is pure, gentle, sane, wise and loving? This is exactly what He is like.

The Holy Spirit is pure, for He is the Holy Spirit. He is wise, for He is the Spirit of wisdom. He is true, for He is the Spirit of truth. He is like Jesus, for He is the Spirit of Christ. He is like the Father, for He is the Spirit of the Father. He wants to be Lord of your life, and He wants to possess you so that you are no longer in command of the little vessel in which you sail. You may be a passenger on board, or one of the crew, but you definitely are not in charge. Someone else is in command of the vessel.

Now, the reason we object to it being that way is because we were born of Adam's corrupted flesh. We want to boss our own lives. That is why I ask: Are you sure that you want to be possessed by the blessed Spirit of the

Father and of the Son? Are you ready and willing for your personality to be taken over by someone who is like this?

He will expect obedience to the written Word of God. But our human problem is that we would like to be full of the Spirit and yet go on and do as we please. The Holy Spirit who inspired the Scriptures will expect obedience to the Scriptures, and if we do not obey the Scriptures, we will quench Him. This Spirit will have obedience—but people do not want to obey the Lord. Everyone is as full as he wants to be. Everyone has as much of God as he desires to have. There is a fugitive impulse that comes to us, in spite of what we ask for when we pray in public, or even in private. We want the thrill of being full, but we don't want to meet the conditions. We just don't want to be filled badly enough to be filled.

Let's use an expensive Cadillac automobile for an illustration. Here is Brother Jones, who would love to drive a Cadillac. But he is not going to buy one, and I will tell you why: He doesn't want a Cadillac badly enough to be willing to pay for it. He does want it—but he doesn't want it with that kind of desire—so he is going to continue to drive his old Chevrolet.

Now, we want to be full—full of the Spirit, but it is not with that kind of extreme desire. So, we settle for something less. We do say, "Lord, I would like to be full, it would be wonderful!" But we are not willing to proceed to meet His terms. We do not want to pay the price. The Holy Spirit will expect obedience to the Word of God.

Then, neither will the Holy Spirit tolerate the self-sins.

What are the self-sins? Start with the love of self, and most of us must confess that we cultivate it. We go to school and learn how to put on and show off. God the Holy Spirit will never allow a Spirit-filled Christian to be like that. He is the Spirit who brings humility to the heart, and that humility will be in evidence or He will be quenched and grieved.

There is also the sin of confidence in self.

We are very sure that we can do very well in our own strength, and the Holy Spirit will want to destroy this kind of self-dependence. You may be a Christian business-man, making all the decisions, buying and selling in big amounts. You go home and run the house and your family. But there is one thing that you will not run, brother —you will not run your own life after the Holy Spirit is given control. You give up the control—the Holy Spirit will lead and direct and control your life, the same as you run your business. You will not be able to dictate to the Holy Spirit. This is our trouble—we are dictators, full of self-confidence.

We need to be reminded that we are full of self-righteousness, too.

Isn't it shocking that Christians can go on continually telling lies to God? Don't we say, "But I am a worm, and no man" (Psalm 22:6)? Don't we get down and say, "For I know that in me (that is, in my flesh,) dwelleth no good thing" (Romans 7:18)? But, if someone called us a liar, our face would turn white and we would say, "What do you mean?" We say that we are bad—but we don't really believe it! God wants to take all of that out of us, my friend. He wants to take Adam's righteousness out of us and put another kind of righteousness within.

He would like to take from our beings selfrighteousness and all of the other self-sins, such as self-indulgence and self-aggrandizement. You have to be sure in your own being whether you want to be treated like that. Are you sure that you want to be filled and possessed by that kind of a Spirit? If you do not desire to be, of course you cannot be. God, through His Holy Spirit, will be gentlemanly—He will not come in where He is not wanted.

Again, do you want to be filled with the Spirit badly enough that you are willing to stand against the easy and dishonest ways of the world and live the hard life of a Christian?

God will want your testimony for Himself alone. He will take the direction of your life away from you altogether, and He will reserve the right to test you and discipline you and strip away from you many of the things that you love.

He will insist upon complete honesty if you are to be filled with the Holy Spirit. Can a Christian brother trim his income tax, and then smile and think that he is getting away with something? No, my brother, you are not getting away with anything—you are just leaking—your spirit is leaking and your soul is leaking. We put things in bags with holes in them and the treasure leaks out. The Holy Spirit will not allow crooked deals, and He will not allow sharp savings.

He will also insist that your days of boasting and showing off are over. God never allowed me to boast about a convert—those I boasted about always backslid, as far as I am able to discover. Every time I boasted about a crowd that listened to me, it always dwindled away. Now I thank God for this, because if I start to show off a little bit, the Lord sets me flat, and that's exactly the way I want to keep it.

Let me warn you about the philosophy that is abroad in Christian circles that says, "I have God and all this, too!" In this twentieth century Western civilization we are rich and well-to-do. We don't really know what it is to be poor, and we don't know what it is to suffer. But I find in the New Testament that the believers had God, and they usually didn't have very much else. Often they had to get rid of what they had for Christ's sake. In the early Church, our fathers knew what it was to suffer and lose things. They paid the price, and we refuse to pay the price.

We read books on the filling of the Spirit, but we won't meet the conditions. We are as full as we want to be. The Scriptures say, "Blessed are they which do hunger and thirst after righteousness: for they shall be filled" (Matthew 5:6). Now, if there is a man anywhere who is hungering after God and is not filled, then the Word of God is broken. We are as full as we want to be.

Do You Really Need *to Be Filled?*

There is another matter that must be settled: You must be sure that you need to be filled with the Spirit.

Why are you interested in this subject? You have received Jesus, you are converted and your sins have been forgiven. You have taken a course in New Testament somewhere. You know that you have eternal life and no man can pluck you out of God's hand. In the meantime, you are having a wonderful time going to heaven.

Are you sure that you can't get along all right the way you are? Do you feel that you just cannot go on resisting discouragement? Do you feel that you cannot obey the Scriptures and understand the truth and bring forth fruit and live in victory without a greater measure of the Holy Spirit than you know now?

If you haven't reached that place, then I don't know that there is much I can do. I wish I could. I wish I could take off the top of your head and pour the holy oil of God down into you—but I can't. I can only do what John the Baptist did when he pointed to Jesus and said, "Behold the Lamb of God, which taketh away the sin of the world" (John 1:29). Then John faded out of the picture. After that, everyone was on his own. Each one had to go to the Lord Jesus Christ and receive help from Christ on his own.

No man can fill me and no man can fill you. We can pray for each other, but I can't fill you and you can't fill me. This desire to be filled must become all-absorbing in your life. If there is anything in your life bigger than your desire to be a Spirit-filled Christian, you will never be a Spirit-filled Christian until that is cured. If there is anything in your life more demanding than your longing after God, then you will never be a Spirit-filled Christian.

I have met Christians who have been wanting to be filled, in a vague sort of way, for many years. The reason they have not been filled with the Spirit is because they have other things they want more. God does not come rushing into a human heart unless He knows that He is the answer and fulfillment to the greatest, most over-powering desire of that life.

Now, right here, let's consider that fact that no one has ever been filled with the Spirit without first having had a time of disturbance and anxiety. We can check this by looking into the scriptural accounts, into post-biblical times, into Church history and biographical accounts of personal experiences of many Christians. I believe that they agree that no one was ever filled with the Spirit without first having a time of disturbance and anxiety.

The Lord's people are like little children—they just want to be happy. They want the Lord to give them a rattle and let them cackle and laugh and be happy. They are going to be happy regardless, but the Lord's happy little children very seldom get filled with the Holy Spirit. God cannot fill them because they are not ready to die to the things upon which they have put their own values. God wants His children to be joyful, but that is not the cheap happiness of the flesh—it is the joy of a resurrected Christ!

It is probably quite generally true that any Christian who has not been filled with the Spirit since his conversion does not have genuine Christian joy. I know this was my experience. I had a lot of joyful feeling when I was first converted. I was a happy Christian. But if this is the kind of happiness that is half carnality and animal spirits, God will want to deliver you from it. To be filled with the Spirit of God is to have come through feelings, disturbance, anxiety, disappointment and emptiness. When you reach that place of despair, when you have gone to the last person and you have written the last editor, when you have followed the last evangelist around and hunted up the last fellow to counsel with you—when no man can help you anymore and you are in a state of inward despair—that is when you will recognize that you are near the place where God can finally do what He wants to do for you. When there comes that despair with self, that emptying out of you and that inner loneliness, you are getting close.

It is part of my belief that God wants to get us to a place where we would still be happy if we had only Him! We don't need God and something else. God does give us Himself and lets us have other things, too, but there is that inner loneliness until we reach the place where it is only God that we desire.

Most of us are too social to be lonely. When we feel

lonely, we rush to the telephone and call Mrs. Yakkety. So we use up thirty minutes, and the buns are burned in the oven. With many, it is talk, talk, talk, and we rush about looking for social fellowship because we cannot stand being alone.

If you will follow on to know the Lord, there comes a place in your Christian life when Mrs. Yakkety will be a pest instead of being a consolation. She won't be able to help you at all. There will not be a thing that she can do for you. It is loneliness for God—you will want God so badly you will be miserable. This means you are getting close, friend. You are near the kingdom, and if you will only keep on, you will meet God. God will take you in and fill you, and He will do it in His own blessed and wonderful way.

Now, take note that this disturbance and anxiety and disappointment and darkness do not "earn" the Holy Spirit for anyone. The Holy Spirit is a gift—a gift from the Father to His children. He is a gift from the wounded side of Jesus to His children. This despair and anxiety does not earn the Spirit for you—what it does do is to break up your fallow ground and empty the human vessel. You cannot be full unless you first are emptied. The anxiety and despair come because you are already too full of many other things. Emptied of these, the blessed Holy Spirit has an opportunity to come in. Moody used to take an empty glass, fill it with water, and then say, "Now, how can I fill this glass with milk?" He would pour it out into another vessel as an object lesson, for there must be an emptying and a detachment from the minor interests of life.

Am I demanding too much as a preacher if I tell you that most of us are far too concerned with the minor things of this life? We are busy making a living so we can die of gallbladder trouble or have a heart attack. We must dash about keeping our sales up and our businesses going. We are Christians, you know, so we just want the Lord to have the chariot ready as we go about killing ourselves off long before our time, and the Lord takes us home to heaven. So we think!

Brethren, is this too rough? Am I demanding too much? I don't think so, for I am probably chilly compared to what I ought to be. I am nowhere nearly as demanding as Finney or John Wesley or many of the great preachers whose appeals God blessed and honored.

HOW TO BE FILLED

Well, these are conditions which must be met, and they are really part of the answer to the question of so many: "How may I be filled with the Holy Spirit of God?"

I am going to give you four Bible passages on how to be filled with the Spirit, and an archangel from heaven could not do better than to give the Scripture to you and say, "Believe the Word of God!"

Present Your Vessel

> I beseech you therefore, brethren, by the mercies of
> God, that ye present your bodies a living sacrifice,
> holy, acceptable unto God, which is your reasonable
> service. And be not conformed to this world: but be
> ye transformed by the renewing of your mind, that
> ye may prove what is that good, and acceptable, and
> perfect, will of God. (Romans 12:1–2)

"Present your bodies . . ."—that is, present your vessel. That must come first. A vessel that has not been presented will not be filled. God cannot fill what He cannot have. Present your vessel.

I think God wants us to be intelligent. He wants us to come to Him. If you were in a bread line in some poor country, and you stood back and would not present your cup, you would not get any milk. And if you did not present the plate or basket, you would not get any bread.

If you will not present your personality, you will not get the fullness of the Spirit of God.

Are you ready to present your body with all of its functions and all that it contains—your mind, your personality, your spirit, your love, your ambitions, your all? This is the first thing. It can be a simple act—presenting the body. Are you willing to do it?

You Must Ask

In Luke 11:11–12 Jesus has said, "If a son shall ask bread of any of you that is a father, will he give him a stone? or if he ask a fish, will he for a fish give him a serpent? Or if he shall ask an egg, will he offer him a scorpion?"

The answer, of course, to each of these questions is "No." So Jesus draws His conclusion: "If ye then, being evil, know how to give good gifts unto your children: how much more shall your heavenly Father give the Holy Spirit to them that ask him?" (Luke 11:13)

God's people all over the world have taken advantage of this gracious offer. They have believed Him—they have asked and they have been filled. "How much more shall your heavenly Father give the Holy Spirit to them that ask him?" (Luke 11:13), so you ask. First, you present your vessel, and then you ask. That is perfectly logical and perfectly clear. I set aside all theological objections to this text. They say that this is not for today.

Let me just ask them why the Lord left us this promise in the Bible. Why didn't He put it somewhere else? Why did He put it where I could see it if He didn't want me to believe it? Oh, it is all for us, and if the Lord wanted to do it, He could give it without our asking, but He chooses to have us ask. "Ask of me, and I shall give thee" (Psalm 2:8) is always God's order. So why not ask?

You Must Be Willingly Obedient

Acts 5:32 points out, "And we are his witnesses of these things; and so is also the Holy Ghost, whom God hath given to them that obey him."

The Spirit of God cannot give a disobedient child His blessing. The Father cannot fill a disobedient child with the Holy Spirit. God gives His Holy Spirit to them that obey Him—those who are obedient to the Word, obedient to the Spirit, obedient to the risen Lord. Are you ready to obey and to do what you are asked to do? What would that be? Simply to live by the Scriptures as you understand them— simple, but revolutionary.

You Must Have Faith in God

"This only would I learn of you, Received ye the Spirit by the works of the law, or by the hearing of faith?" (Galatians 3:2).

Now the answer is, of course, by the hearing of faith.

He said, "Are ye so foolish? having begun in the Spirit, are ye now made perfect by the flesh?" (3:3). You are not filled with the Holy Spirit by law-keeping. You are filled with the Holy Spirit by faith and obedience to your Lord. I am talking about His coming and possessing the full body and mind and life and being, taking over the entire personality, directly but gently making it His, so that we may become a habitation of God through the Spirit.

Now, let us sum up what we have said. Every Christian has a measure of the Holy Spirit and do not let anyone argue you out of that. "Now if any man have not the Spirit of Christ, he is none of his" (Romans 8:9), and so He has given us a deposit of the Holy Spirit.

We have been considering the filling and the fullness and the anointing of the Holy Spirit. The word "anointing" is what I want to emphasize at this point. The anointing is not a gradual thing. "Anointing" is an Old Testament word and an act accomplished by pouring oil on an individual's head. When they poured oil on a man's head, it was not a gradual process—when they poured the oil they turned the thing over and poured it out, and it ran all over and down the skirts of his garment. Everyone for a quarter of a mile around knew that the oil had been poured upon him because it was the oil of frankincense and myrrh and aloes and cassia and cinnamon. It perfumed everything around with a beautiful fragrance, and it didn't happen gradually. It happened instantaneously. Our problem is that we do not want to go through the experience of being filled with the Spirit. We want to be blessed, to go to heaven, wear a crown and rule over five cities.

We do not want to come to that place where the Lord chops us down and hews us up. We don't want that! That is why we are the weak people that we are these days. The Lord's people want Jesus to do all the dying, and they want to do all the chuckling.

Perhaps our greatest shame is that we do not want to know what the cross really means!

O, Cross that liftest up my head, I dare not ask to fly
  from Thee;
I lay in dust, life's glory dead,
And from the ground there blossoms red
  Life that shall endless be.

Albert L. Peace, "O Love That Wilt Not Let Me Go," Hymns of the Christian Life (Camp Hill, PA: Christian Publications, 1978), # 181, verse 4.

CHAPTER 6

———————•———————

Do You Have All God Wants for You?

And, behold, I send the promise of my Father upon you: but tarry ye in the city of Jerusalem, until ye be endued with power from on high.

LUKE 24:49

For John truly baptized with water; but ye shall be baptized with the Holy Ghost not many days hence.

ACTS 1:5

It is my contention that the individual believers who comprise the membership of our evangelical Christian churches ought to be leading fruitful and happy Spirit-filled lives.

If you will set aside the necessary time to search the Scriptures with an honest and open being, you will be convinced that fruitfulness and joy and peace and blessing and contentment are all part and parcel of what the

Holy Spirit expects to provide in and through the yielded life of the Christian believer.

Now, I know that some say that I have confused people about the blessing of the Holy Spirit, and in answer I want to point out that if the Lord's people were only half as eager to be filled with the Spirit, the Church would be crowded out.

I have never tried to bend people to the working of God merely by eloquence, for if I don't teach according to the truth found in the Bible, I'm wrong no matter how eloquent I try to be.

But in these matters, I have spent a long time in the Word of God myself, and I can speak with a good deal of authority because I have gone through it, and I know what I'm speaking about. However, I wouldn't ever try to push one of God's children into any knowledge or any experience, because I have found that we try to push too much and too soon. We only result in kicking God's children out of their shells too soon, and as a result, we have a lot of weird monstrosities instead of saints. I don't want to do that!

I can only wonder why it is that Christian people can go on and on and not be concerned about actually lacking the blessings and gifts promised by a loving Father in heaven.

As a Christian believer, shouldn't my life and outlook, and the very life of my church, be affected by the promise of the Father God that He would give the Spirit as a gift to His children?

In Luke 11:13 I am sure God had in mind the love we have for our children when He said, "If ye then, being evil, know how to give good gifts unto your children: how much more shall your heavenly Father give the Holy Spirit to them that ask him?"

NOTHING TO FEAR

In making the Spirit the promise of the Father, I believe God wanted to show that we don't have to be afraid of the Holy Spirit. I say this because I have found that it is very difficult to get Christians over the fear of the Holy Spirit. Just remember that He is given to us as the Father's promised gift. If a man promises his son a beautiful bicycle for Christmas, the son is certainly never afraid of the promise made by a father who loves him and wants to provide the best for him.

The members of the redeemed Church should be bound into a bundle of love with the Holy Spirit. The truth is that God never fathered His Church apart from the Holy Spirit. We should be anointed with the Spirit. We are led of the Spirit. We are taught by the Spirit. The Spirit, then, is the medium, the divine solution, in which God holds His Church.

The Bible plainly indicates that God never dreamed of His people apart from the Holy Spirit. Actually, He made many promises to them based on the coming of the Spirit.

Let's note some of the promises He made. In Isaiah 32:15–17, He said:

Until the spirit be poured upon us from on high, and the wilderness be a fruitful field, and the fruitful field be counted for a forest. Then judgment shall dwell in the wilderness, and righteousness . . . shall be peace; and the effect of righteousness quietness and assurance for ever.

Farther on, in Isaiah 44:3, He said:

For I will pour water upon him that is thirsty, and floods upon the dry ground: I will pour my spirit upon thy seed, and my blessing upon thine offspring.

There is also that passage in Joel 2:28–29:

And it shall come to pass afterward, that I will pour out my spirit upon all flesh; and your sons and your daughters shall prophesy, your old men shall dream dreams, your young men shall see visions: And also upon the servants and upon the handmaids in those days will I pour out my spirit.

Now, those were the words of the Father, and Jesus interpreted them and called them the "promise of the Father" (Acts 1:4). Let me say that whenever you read about Jesus, our Lord, interpreting the Old Testament, you stay close by His interpretation. Don't lean too hard on the interpretations of men, because they can be wrong.

Our Lord, the man Christ Jesus, never was wrong—and He called this the "promise of the Father."

Recall that in Luke 24:49, Jesus said, "I send the promise of my Father upon you: but tarry ye . . . until ye be endued with power." Now, I say that Jesus further interpreted this in chapters 14, 15 and 16 of the Gospel of John, as He talked about the Holy Spirit and His coming to the Church.

THREE DISCERNIBLE PERIODS

Here I should point out that in reading the Gospels, the book of Acts and the Epistles, we can easily trace three periods that are discernible with respect to the Holy Spirit and His work in the Church.

The Promise

First is what we may call *the period of the promise*, from the time of John the Baptist to the resurrection of Christ. In this three-year period, the disciples were called, commissioned and taught in the best Bible school in the world, for there isn't a seminary on earth that can equal the seminary in which Jesus was the entire faculty! They didn't get a degree which they could frame and put on the wall, but they had a degree inside of them, and they loved Christ, our Lord. They loved Him living, they loved Him dead, and they loved Him living again.

Now at that time they had only been promised something. Jesus had told them and taught them that there was a new kind of life coming to them—not poetic, not psychic and not physical.

It was to be an afflatus from above. It was to be something that was to come to them out of the world beyond them, over the threshold of their beings, into the *sanctum sanctorum*, into the deep of their spirits. The Counselor would live there and teach them and lead them and make them holy and give them power.

Jesus taught that all the way through!

As He came nearer to the end of His earthly life, He intensified this teaching as revealed in John 14, 15 and 16. He told them that there was a new and superior kind of life coming, and He told them that it was to be an infusion, an outpouring of spiritual energy. Then He left them.

Do you know that if we could get together today a congregation as spiritually minded as the disciples were before Pentecost, we would feel that we had an intensely spiritual church? We would make bishops out of the leadership of that kind of group. We would elect them to boards and write the stories of their lives and name churches after them.

But in that period of promise, the disciples were just getting ready. They had not yet received the promise. Jesus was creating an expectation within them.

The Preparation

The second period outlined is *the period of preparation*. In some measure, they were being prepared while Jesus was with them, but after He was gone, they actually began to prepare. They stopped their activities, and this is one of the great lessons for us in our hectic day.

I think we are the busiest bunch of eager beavers ever seen in the religious world. The idea seems to be that if we are not running in a circle, breathing down the back of our own neck, we are not pleasing God!

When Jesus said, "Go ye into all the world, and preach the gospel to every creature" (Mark 16:15), Peter probably leaped to his feet and, no doubt, scooped up his hat on the way out. He was going to go right then!

But the Lord said, Peter, come back, and "tarry ye in the city of Jerusalem, until ye be endued with power from on high" (Luke 24:49).

I heard a Christian leader warn recently that we are suffering from a rash of amateurism in Christian circles. Christianity has leveled down and down and down. We are as light as butterflies—though we flit, flit, flit around in the sunshine and imagine that we are eagles flapping our broad wings.

Sometimes I think the Church would be better off if we would call a moratorium on activity for about six weeks and just wait on God to see what He is waiting to do for us. That's what they did before Pentecost. We spend time praying for the Holy Spirit to unite us, but at Pentecost the Spirit of God came upon the disciples because they were already united—"they were all with one accord in one place" (Acts 2:1).

Many are trying to work for God when they are not really prepared to work. There needs to be some preparation, some getting ready. I think we often make mistakes with our newest converts. We think nothing of taking one of our babes in Christ, pushing a bunch of tracts into his hands, and saying, "Now, Bud, get going!" Perhaps we ought not to forget that in the Old Testament the priests in the service of God were born priests but they had to be anointed before they could serve. Not only was blood placed on their ears, on their thumbs and toes, but fragrant sweet oil, the type of the Holy Spirit, was put on the blood.

The Realization

The third period indicated was that of *the period of realization*, and I read that the Holy Spirit came upon them suddenly.

I have noted that this word "suddenly," as found in the book of Acts, occurs often in places in the Scriptures.

"And suddenly there came a sound from heaven as of a rushing mighty wind, and it filled all the house where they were sitting" (2:2). I have to smile to myself because of that word "suddenly." God's people in our day are so afraid of the implications of "suddenly."

Most of us in the Church want things to slip up on us gradually, a little bit at a time—slowly, not suddenly. Everyone is willing to be filled with the Holy Spirit providing God does it very gingerly, very slowly, and doesn't embarrass or frighten them!

The Scriptures say that "Suddenly. . . . They were all filled with the Holy Ghost" (2:2, 4). The Scriptures also declare that "And suddenly there was with the angel a multitude of the heavenly host praising God" (Luke 2:13). It is amazing that we will find the word "suddenly" whenever God did a wonderful thing. He did it suddenly—but we are afraid of that. We want to "grow" in grace because we know that we can grow and not be embarrassed.

It seems to be an embarrassment to believers to get down on their knees to seek Almighty God, to have to get out a handkerchief to wipe away the tears and then to find themselves saying, "Thank God, the Counselor has come!" It might take something away from their reputation—chairman of the board, Sunday school teachers, workers in the ladies' aid.

The result of this kind of embarrassment is that we go on year after year and learn to live with death. We find ourselves able to live with a spiritual corpse. Our breath is frosty, our cheeks are pale, our toes are frostbitten and we haven't any spirituality. We learn to live with that—and we imagine that is "normal." We even write books to prove that it is normal, but the Holy Spirit isn't on us, and that's our trouble.

The period of the realization came suddenly, and the Father fulfilled His promise. The expectations were fully met and more!

AN ERROR IN THE CHURCH

I am concerned about anything that hinders God's people and keeps them from their full privileges in the Christian life. Sometimes I have to tear into things that I cannot believe are right, and which I feel become a hindrance to the people of God. Some have said that it is none of my business, but it is my business. I have been anointed of God to make this concern my business!

One of these things is an error often presented to the Church in this form: that the individual Christian is not concerned with this promise by the Father that He would send the Holy Spirit, that this already happened once in the Christian Church and that it is not to be repeated. Therefore, this position holds that the Church need no longer be concerned about the Holy Spirit. So, they try to brush us off.

Well, here I would like to ask you some questions and let you do your own teaching as you answer them.

Is it true that the Father's promise was valid only to the Christians of the first century?

I think we are living in the period of the "last days," which began with Pentecost and continues until Christ returns. That makes the Prophet Joel's text active and efficacious and applicable to you and me. We are now living in the latter days when God will pour out His Spirit on all flesh.

Recall what Peter said in Acts 2:38–39:

> Then Peter said unto them, Repent, and be baptized
> every one of you in the name of Jesus Christ for
> the remission of sins, and ye shall receive the gift of
> the Holy Ghost. For the promise is unto you, and
> to your children, and to all that are afar off, even as
> many as the Lord our God shall call.

It wasn't just that first generation crowd—"unto you,
and to your children, and to all that are afar off" (2:39)—
that's the promise. Many of us believe and know the witness of the Spirit—and this takes the place of a lot of argument. If you can argue a man into believing he is filled,
someone else will come along who can argue him out of
believing that he is filled. I point to the Lamb of God
that takes away the sins of the world and the promise
of the Father for a holy and fruitful life in the Spirit—if
anything happens to me, he will have the promise of the
Father. He won't be cast back on man's uncertainty.

A second question: Does the new birth of the first
century make my new birth unnecessary?

The Lord said that we would have to be born again,
and He said we were to be filled with the Spirit. Yet someone comes along and tells us that what it really means is

that *they* were to be filled with the Spirit back there—and not us.

That leaves us high and dry hanging on a wire, without any hope, born a long time too late. But, wait! Peter was born again. Does Peter's experience of being born again suffice for me? Peter was filled with the Spirit. Does Peter's being filled with the Spirit suffice for me? Would the breakfast that Peter ate in AD 33 nourish and suffice me in the twentieth century?

No, of course not. I have to eat now if I'm going to be nourished now. Peter's being born again won't help me now. I must be born again as he was born again then. Peter's being filled that day won't help me now. I must be filled now as he was filled then. Is there any difference between that and the outpouring of the Spirit?

A third question: Have you ever seen anyone in the Christian Church today that received at conversion what Peter received in the upper chamber?

I am asking this because some would teach that we now receive at conversion what the disciples received back there at Pentecost.

When you were converted, did you have the power Peter had when he was filled? Bring it down farther—down to the common folk around Peter. Doesn't the Scripture make it pretty plain that they received something and had something that we apparently don't have in this day in which we live? I think they did!

Now a final question: Is modern fundamental belief a satisfactory fulfillment of the expectation raised by the Father in Christ, and does your heart personally witness that what you now enjoy is what our Lord promised to His people?

Brethren, our heavenly Father promised the gift of the Holy Spirit to come upon His children. Jesus Himself promised that we should have the Spirit, that He would take the things of Christ and make them known to us, and that we should have power from on high.

Now, I look around at cold, dead, dried-up, fundamental textualism hanging out to dry. Then they want me to believe that what they have now is what those early Christians had back there. I just can't believe it!

They were thoroughbreds in those early days. Something from God had come to them, and they blazed with light and power and life. Most of us are "scrubs" compared with those early-day Christians. When I was a boy on the farm in Pennsylvania, we had scrub chickens. Occasionally, my mother would try to improve the strain, bringing in some Plymouth Rocks or some other good breed. But just let the hens go awhile. In five or six years, they will revert back to type. They will go back to scrubs, and you can't figure out what they are—just old, dried-up clucking biddies that lay little eggs, and not too many of them!

We Christians have just reverted back to old Adamic type. Just look at us, and then try to say that we automatically have the same spiritual life of those thoroughbreds. Think it over!

Do you have the witness in your being now that what you possess in spiritual life and victory is all God meant when He painted that wonderful picture of the fullness of the Spirit?

A MODERN TESTIMONY

Let me remind you of Mother Cook, a nice little old lady who lived in her modest home on Chicago's South Side and who knew the blessing of the fullness of the Holy Spirit.

A young man got converted in this city, and he would have made a good salesman. He was very busy—he loved to run in circles, and he did. He went everywhere running in circles, and his name was Dwight Lyman Moody.

One day Mother Cook saw Dwight and said, "Son, I'd like to have you come over to my house sometime—I want to talk to you." So Moody went over, and she set him down on a chair and said something to this general effect:

"Now, Dwight, it's wonderful to see you saved so wonderfully and to see your zeal for the Lord, but do you know what you need? You need to be anointed with the Holy Spirit."

"Well," he said, "Mother Cook, I want whatever God has for me."

"All right," she said, "get down here." So he knelt down on the linoleum, and they prayed. Mother Cook prayed, "Oh, God, fill this young man with Thine own Spirit."

Moody died out right there, opened his heart, yielded himself as an empty vessel and took the promise by faith —but nothing happened. But a few days afterward, he was in another city, and he said, "As I was walking down the street, *suddenly* God fulfilled the promise He had made to me in that kitchen."

Down into him came a horn of oil, and the Holy Spirit came on him. He said he turned up an alley and raised his hand and said, "Oh, God, stay Your power, or I'll die!"

Later he said, "I went out from there preaching the same sermons with the same texts, but oh, the difference now—the Holy Spirit had come!"

Yes, the Holy Spirit had been there. The Holy Spirit was there causing him to be born again, for "Now if any man have not the Spirit of Christ, he is none of his" (Romans 8:9).

But it is quite a different thing to have the Spirit as the agent in my regeneration than to have the horn of oil poured out on my head—quite a different thing—and that was Moody's testimony and appeal concerning the fullness of the Holy Spirit.

Where did we get this idea that because the disciples were filled with the Spirit back there in the first century, it is unnecessary for us to be filled with the Spirit now?

There was a time when the Holy Spirit came upon the Church, and it went forth in a blaze of fire to preach the gospel to the known world in the first 100 years.

Then came the long death.

Now, here we are in our time, and we have teachers who are so infinitely silly as to tell us that all we have to do is just go quietly along until the Lord comes and makes us to rule over many cities. I only ask that you search the Scriptures and see whether these things be so. Pray and yield and believe and obey—and see what God will do for you!

CHAPTER 7

Spiritual Gifts: The Ability to Do

Now concerning spiritual gifts, brethren,
I would not have you ignorant.

1 CORINTHIANS 12:1

But unto every one of us is given grace according
to the measure of the gift of Christ.

EPHESIANS 4:7

For I say, through the grace given unto me, to every man that is
among you, not to think of himself more highly than he ought
to think; but to think soberly, according as God hath dealt to
every man the measure of faith. For as we have many members
in one body, and all members have not the same office: so we,
being many, are one body in Christ, and every one members one
of another. Having then gifts differing according to the grace that
is given to us, whether prophecy, let us prophesy according to the
proportion of faith; or ministry, let us wait on our ministering:
or he that teacheth, on teaching; or he that exhorteth, on
exhortation: he that giveth, let him do it with simplicity; he that
ruleth, with diligence; he that sheweth mercy, with cheerfulness.

ROMANS 12:3–8

Nothing in the whole world is quite so wonderfully made as the human body, and it is small wonder that the Holy Spirit said through David, "I am fearfully and wonderfully made" (Psalm 139:14). The hands, the ears, the sense of smell, the sense of taste, the sense of touch, feet and hands all working together—only the creative wisdom and power of God can account for the amazing human body.

I call your attention to the fact that in three of his epistles, the apostle Paul used the members of the physical body to illustrate the spiritual relationships in the Body of Christ, the Church. He used the body-member relationship in Romans, in First Corinthians and in Ephesians.

In Romans 12, Paul, being a great illustrator, broke things down for us so that we could easily understand when he said that the Church is a body—Christ is the head and the true Christian is a member of that body.

Now the Holy Spirit is to the Church what your spirit is to the body which God has given you. It is the life, the union, the consciousness—and as each member recapitulates the local church, each local church recapitulates the entire Church of Christ, Paul asserts.

ALL ONE BODY

What Paul is emphasizing is the fact that the Church, the Body of Christ, is not torn nor divided, but each local church group has all the functions of the whole body. Just as each individual state is a vital, throbbing part of the whole union of the states, so each local church is a living, organic part of the whole Church of Christ. I believe that we are members of the whole Body of Christ in heaven and all over the world, but we are all descendants of the great God, who by the Holy Spirit and the Word caused us to be born into His family.

Therefore, the Church of Christ is not divided. When we sing that old song, "We are not divided, all one body we," people smile and say, "How about your 600 denominations?"

Well, they don't frustrate me with that question. That song, that truth—"We are not divided, all one body we"—is just as true as the fact that I am not divided. The Body of Christ is all one body. We can sing it, and let those people make fun of us if they will—keep on singing it, for it is true!

We are not divided. It is a whole Church. Everyone who has ever been born into the family of God is born into a living, organic union, and there we are. There is nothing the devil can do about it.

Each local group, I say, has all the functions of the whole group, just as the body of each man has all of the human faculties and organs and members. The members are designed so that each has a function. The eyes are designed to see, the ears to hear, the hands to do work, the feet for movement, the stomach to digest food, and so on.

So, we are designed to cooperate, and that's in concert. I remember once reading a great article in *Harper's* magazine. It explained what brought on old age. It said it was not the loss of strength in any organ of the body, but that the organs of the body ceased to cooperate and went off on their own, and that was what brought on old age. It was the failure of the organs of the body to cooperate that made people die of old age. They got independent and went off and started their own tabernacle, if we can use it in that sense of illustration!

So it is with the Church. When we work together and have a sense of unity and fellowship, when we all work together, cooperate with each other and act in concert, when all are for each and each for all, and all take directions from the Head, then one has a perfect Church. Each local church can sum it up, and we can all sum it up ourselves.

THE GIFTS OF THE HOLY SPIRIT

Anything that God can do through all of His Church, He can do through a local church, a local group. These various functions are the abilities to work and they are called gifts. He said, "Having then gifts differing according to the grace that is given to us" (Romans 12:6a), "Now concerning spiritual gifts, brethren" (1 Corinthians 12:1a), "But covet earnestly the best gifts" (12:31a), "When he ascended up on high, he . . . gave gifts unto men" (Ephesians 4:8).

So, when the gifts are lodged in the Body of Christ, in the local church, they are the ability to do. By way of illustration, your stomach is a gift from God. The purpose of it is not to hold up your trousers, just something to put a belt around. The stomach has a purpose and a function. What is your liver for? What are your eyes for? They have specific purposes and functions, something to do and accomplish. If they do their function and all the others cooperate, you will be a healthy, useful person.

We have these gifts in the Church in the same manner. Paul said in his careful instructions in the God-inspired writings that these gifts are placed to get things done. They exist in the Church for a purpose.

Now, Paul also used sports to illustrate, so if I use sports to illustrate, don't say I'm not spiritual. I have no ambition to be more spiritual than the apostle Paul! You know that a baseball team in action has nine men. There's a fellow to catch the ball, there's a fellow to pitch the ball, there's a fellow in center field, and there's a fellow on first base and second base, etc. Each man in his own position has a function, and each knows what he is to do. As long as he does his job skillfully, the team as a unit is hard to beat. Whenever a team gets a star who does not care whether the team wins or not, provided he can shine, the success of the team as a winning unit is sacrificed.

Paul says that these gifts are in the Body. Some say that there are only nine, because the opening verses of First Corinthians list nine. But do you know that I have counted at least eighteen in the Scriptures? There may be some that overlap, and the list could be reduced to fifteen. Let me follow the Scriptures closely now and staying by the Word of God, let me simply name the gift functions of the divine Body which are named by Paul.

First, there is the gift of an apostle, or an ambassador or messenger. There is the gift that makes a prophet. There is the gift that makes a teacher. Then, there is the gift that makes an exhorter. There is the gift that makes the ruler. That would be someone like the old Presbyterians called a ruling elder. Then there are the gifts of wisdom, of knowledge, of faith, of healing. There is a gift of miracles, a gift of tongues, a gift of interpretation, a gift of discernment, a gift of helps, a gift of mercy showing, a gift of government, a gift of liberality and the gift of the evangelist.

There you have it. These are the gifts which are in the Body, the functions which enable the Holy Spirit to work. As long as you have the bodily members, the life within you can find its mode of expression.

As long as your hands are obedient to the head, they will be all right. Just as long as your feet take orders from the head, you will not get hit as you cross the street. Just as long as the members of your body do their work and take orders from the head, you will be all right. Just as long as the Church of Christ recognizes the Lord as being the Head of the Church, and Christians as members in particular and these members gifted with "abilities to do," we will have a revived and blessed Church!

WHEN THE GIFTS ARE MISSING

Remember that the work of the Church is done by the Spirit, working through these gifts and through these gifted members. Where these gifts are not present, or not recognized, or denied, the Church is thrown back upon other ways of getting a work done.

There are several mistaken emphases in our circles, and the first is just plain humanism. If you had no hands, you would have to do the best you could without hands. If you had no eyes, you would be doing the best you could without eyes. If you had no feet, you would have to crawl around as well as you could without feet. So, if we deny or refuse to recognize that there are members, and that there are gifts in these members, then we are thrown back upon mere humanism. We have this in great measure today. We are thrown back upon talent—just talent. Let me solemnly tell you that the Holy Spirit never works with mere talent. Don't be mistaken by the parable where Jesus uses the word *talent*, which was a sum of money (see Matthew 25:14–30). It had no reference to the ability to sing or imitate or project—whatever it is that theatrical people do with their talent.

Our second mistake is that we are thrown back upon psychology as a substitute. I am quite amused and somewhat disgusted with some of my ministerial brethren who are so busy studying psychology in order to know how to handle their congregations. When you have a Bible and a mind, a mouth and the Holy Spirit, why do you have to study psychology? I recall my own experience as a young fellow when I thought it necessary to become a great student of psychology. I studied Watson and James, and particularly Freud, who was the father of psychiatry and psychoanalysis. I learned all the terms and all the pitch. I'm not dumb about psychology, but there is no use bringing psychology to the pulpit when you have the Holy Spirit. If you have the gift of the Spirit, you do not need to study Freud. If you do study him, that is all right, but don't bring him to the pulpit with you!

Another mistake we make is dependence on business methods. I get amused and hurt a little about these brethren and their business methods, trying to carry on the work of God after the fashion of the American businessman. When we carry on the way they do on Madison Avenue or Wall Street, the body is all artificial limbs. It won't work!

Then there is the political technique, with persuasion by sales methods. I think we are going to have to restudy this whole teaching of the place of the Holy Spirit in the Church, so the Body can operate again. If the life goes out of a man's body, he is said to be a corpse. He is what they call "the remains." It is sad, but humorously sad, that a strong, fine man with shining eyes and vibrant voice, a living man, dies, and we say, "the remains" can be seen at a funeral home. All the remains of the man, and the least part about him, is what you can see there in the funeral home. The living man is gone. You have only the body. The body is "the remains."

NO LIFE WITHOUT THE SPIRIT

So it is in the Church of Christ. It is literally true that some churches are dead. The Holy Spirit has gone out of them and all you have left are "the remains." You have the potential of the church but you do not have the church, just as you have in a dead man the potential of a living man but you do not have a living man. He can't talk, he can't taste, he can't touch, he can't feel, he can't smell, he can't see, he can't hear—because he is dead! The soul has gone out of the man, and when the Holy Spirit is not present in the Church, you have to get along after the methods of business or politics or psychology or human effort.

You cannot overstate the necessity for the Holy Spirit in the Church, if you say it according to the Scriptures, for without the Spirit there can be nothing done for eternity. Someone will say, "If that's true, why don't we just cast our lot in with the tongues movement, because they believe you can be sure you are filled with the Spirit, but you must have the evidence of tongues"?

Well, in answer, I have known and studied these dear brethren, and I have preached to them for a long, long time. I have studied them, and I know them very well, and I am very sympathetic with them. There are some churches that are very sane and very beautiful and godly.

I don't want to hurt anyone's feelings, but it is true that, as Christians, we have to smile and thank God for the truth, whether it hurts or not. The movement itself has magnified one single gift above all others, and that one gift is the one Paul said was the least. An unscriptural exhibition of that gift results, and there is a tendency to place personal feeling above the Scriptures, and we must never, never do that!

God has given us the Book, brother, and the Book comes first. If it can't be shown in the Book, then I don't want anyone coming to me all aquiver and trying to tell me anything. The Book—you must give me the Word!

Another direction of teaching in our day is this: Some brethren say that the gifts of the Spirit ceased when the apostles died. With the death of the apostles, there are no gifts of the Spirit, they declare.

Now, here we have two directions: The first teaching that before you can be sure you are filled with the Spirit you must have the evidence of tongues; the other, that in these days all gifts are canceled and dead and not available in the Church.

EXAMPLES FROM HISTORY

How are we going to find our way around in all this? Let me remind you of certain people who lived and served God and some of the things they did. Let us see how either of these two extremes answer these exploits for God.

Take Augustine, for instance, the Bishop of Hippo, that saintly man who walked with God and wrote a great confession of faith. There is more of God in Augustine's *Confessions* than there is in all of the books written in fundamental circles in the last fifty years. If I were on an island and I could have a pile of all the fundamental, full-gospel literature written in the last fifty years, or have Augustine's *Confessions*, I would give up all the rest to keep the one book because God is in that book! He's the man who was a great orator and a great student of Greek oratory. When he was filled with the Holy Spirit, he said, "I lost my taste for Greek oratory and it bothered me. Later on I discovered why. I found not Christ in the Greek orator." He was one of the six great brains of all times and he gave it all up that he might follow Christ.

Consider Bernard of Cluny, also. Bernard of Cluny was a saint, and he wrote *Jerusalem the Golden.* You remember that great thing, "Jerusalem, the golden, with milk and honey blest." This man walked with God. He had a twin, Bernard of Clairvaux, who wrote, "Jesus, the very thought of Thee with sweetness fills my breast" and other such beautiful and wonderful hymns.

Then there was Richard Rolle, who lived in the fourteenth century. He was a monk, but he got so blessed he couldn't stay in the monastery, so he got himself a guitar and went all over England preaching the gospel he called "Heat, fragrance and song." It was hot, it was sweet and it was music.

There was Brother Lawrence, the man who practiced the presence of God. He wouldn't pick up a straw from the ground but for the love of God. When he was dying, they said, "What are you doing, Brother Lawrence?" He said, "I'm doing what I plan to do through all eternity—worship God. When I die I won't change my occupation. I have just been worshiping God for forty years on earth, and when I get to heaven I'll just keep right on doing what I am doing."

Recall, too, Thomas à Kempis who wrote *The Imitation of Christ*, and that man they called Dr. Martin Luther, who said, "I'm going to get married to tease the pope and to make the devil mad." He was the man who stood and said, "If every tile on the housetop was a devil, here I stand. I can do nothing else, so help me God!" He gave the Word of God back to the Church and put the pope in his place.

Zinzendorf was that rich, German nobleman who saw a painting of Christ crucified on the cross. He wept and said, "If He died for me, I must give myself to Him!" Out of his devotion and vision came the emphasis from which all of the great missionary movements of the present day have sprung.

There was Tersteegen, a silk weaver in Germany who had such an experience with God that he signed a covenant with God in his own blood. His cottage became a center of spiritual power for all of Germany.

John Newton wrote "How Sweet the Name of Jesus Sounds." This wonderful man was a dealer of slaves in

Africa and yet was converted and became one of the most blazing saints of his generation.

How would we get along without the works of Charles Wesley? His "Jesus, Lover of My Soul," "Love Divine, All Loves Excelling," and his "And Can It Be That I Should Gain an Interest in the Saviour's Blood?" are just a few. And his brother, John Wesley, the man who was an egg catcher, for they threw barrels of eggs at him, you know! He went right on preaching until he changed the whole moral complexion of England. The historians said that he saved England from a revolution. Consider William Booth, who started the Salvation Army, or Jonathan Edwards, the great American preacher who brought the great revival—a great awakening. Think of Frederick Faber, who wrote "Oh, Jesus, Jesus, dearest Lord, forgive me if I say, for very love, Thy sacred Name a thousand times a day"; and Reginald Heber, the Anglican, who wrote "Holy, Holy, Holy, Lord God Almighty."

In our own country there was Charles Finney, the law-yer who was converted and filled with the Holy Spirit, so that he said, "The Holy Spirit descended upon me in a manner that seemed to go through me, body and soul. I could feel the impression like a wave of electricity going through and through me. Indeed, it seemed to come in waves and waves of liquid love . . . like the very breath of God . . . it seemed to fan me like immense wings." Recall with me David Livingstone, who opened Africa to the gospel; and Charles Spurgeon, who preached to 6,000 persons in London every Sunday for a lifetime. It was said of Spurgeon that his prayers healed more sick people in London than all the doctors put together.

George Mueller went to England and opened an orphanage at Bristol. This man prayed down millions of dollars into his hands and blessed thousands of people and brought up thousands of orphans, and God never refused him anything. Think of Frances Havergal, of whom it was said that when she came into a room, there was a consciousness of two people coming into the room— Frances Havergal and the Holy Spirit.

Evan Roberts was the man who prayed, "Bend me, oh God, bend me!" and God bent him and gave Wales its great revival. Dr. Seng, the Chinese Christian who was beaten and sewed in a sack and bruised and kicked about, went out and preached up and down China, and God came on him with great miracles and wonders.

Dr. A. B. Simpson started out with eight people who prayed for missions, and now we remember him as the founder of the sixth largest missionary society in the world.

Billy Nicholson, dear old Billy, who went to be with his Lord not so very long ago, was the evangelist who came to Ireland at a time of political unrest and moral decadence. So many people were converted under Billy Nicholson that a revolution was avoided.

Did you ever hear of the Irish-Canadian woman who was called Holy Ann? They said Holy Ann talked about her Father so intimately that you would think that God had no other children but her. Have you read the life of Sammy Morris? I never saw Sammy Morris myself, but I once stood with bared head beside his grave. Sammy Morris, the Kru boy from Africa, who heard about the Holy Spirit and came to the United States. He worked his way here to talk to somebody who could tell him about the Holy Spirit. Someone took him around New York City and said, "Look at this building, look at that building." Sammy Morris broke in and said, "I haven't come to New York to look at buildings. Do you know anything about the Holy Spirit?" He went on to Taylor University and said, "I understand you Methodists believe in the Holy Spirit, and I want to know more about Him. If you have a room anywhere up under the edge of the roof that no other student will take, that's the one I want." Sammy Morris, a reflection of Christ, lived only a short time. He lies buried in the city of Fort Wayne, Indiana, where I stood beside his grave.

I can name only a few—reams of paper would have to be used to write just the names of the great saints who have lived and have rocked and shaken nations and have cleaned up cities and towns. Revivals now come and go and leave the communities unchanged. Revivals in those days left the imprint of God.

HOW DID THEY DO IT?

Now, for those who say that the gifts died with the apostles: If the gifts of the Spirit died with the apostles, how did Augustine, Bernard of Cluny, Richard Rolle, Brother Lawrence, Thomas à Kempis, Luther, Zinzendorf, Tersteegen, William Booth, Jonathan Edwards, Charles Finney, Charles Spurgeon, George Mueller, A. B. Simpson, Billy Nicholson, Holy Ann and Sammy Morris perform the works of God? How did they do it? If the Holy Spirit has no gifts for men, did they do it by their intellect, did they do it by their brains? No, my brethren, these were men and women of gifts, and the gifts were in them, and the Spirit of God used them mightily, working through them as my soul works through my hands.

On the other side, if we are not filled with the Spirit unless we have the evidence of tongues, then Augustine, Bernard, Thomas à Kempis, Frederick Faber, Charles Finney, David Livingstone, Charles Spurgeon and George Mueller weren't filled with the Holy Spirit. Not one of them ever said anything about the evidence of tongues. Can we say they wrought their mighty, world-changing deeds in the power of the flesh? Oh no, brother! I don't go along with either extreme. I know that the gifts of the Spirit did not die with the apostles. I know that there are gifts today in the Christian Church, even in some churches that don't know they have them.

We cannot help ourselves by going somewhere else or joining something new. Brother, you don't get help by going out somewhere and "joining" something. God is not looking for tags nor titles nor names! He is looking for people. He is looking for loving, humble, clean people, and if He can find such people, He is prepared to move in at once with great power.

"But ye shall receive power" (Acts 1:8). "But covet earnestly the best gifts" (1 Corinthians 12:31). Anything that God has ever done for a soul He will do for anyone else, if the conditions are met. The Lord who blessed these men that I spoke about, and the thousands who followed them but whose names are not known, is willing to do the same for us as He did for them.

FAITH OR UNBELIEF

Unbelief says: Some other time, but not now; some other place, but not here; some other people, but not us. Faith says: Anything He did anywhere else He will do here; anything He did any other time He is willing to do now; anything He ever did for other people He is willing to do for us! With our feet on the ground, and our head cool, but with our heart ablaze with the love of God, we walk out in this fullness of the Spirit, if we will yield and obey. God wants to work through you!

The Counselor has come, and He doesn't care about the limits of locality, geography, time or nationality. The Body of Christ is bigger than all of these. The question is: Will you open your heart?

When Noah sent forth the dove, and she could find no place to land, he "put forth his hand, and took her, and pulled her in unto him into the ark" (Genesis 8:9). If I could fall back on that little illustration, would you reach out your hand by faith and pull the Holy Spirit in unto you? It would make a great and wonderful difference in your life. I've seen it happen and there's no reason why it can't happen for you if you fully obey.

———————•———————

CHAPTER 8

Cultivating the Fellowship of the Holy Spirit

Can two walk together, except they be agreed?

AMOS 3:3

Contrary to what professing Christians like to think, many of God's people are not willing to walk in perfect agreement with Him, and this may explain why so many believers do not have the power of the Spirit, the peace of the Spirit and many of the other qualities, gifts and benefits which the Spirit of God brings.

The question is, are we willing to walk with Him in love and obedience?

The answer is that we cannot walk with Him unless we are agreed; and if we are not agreed, we will not walk with Him in harmony and fruitfulness and blessing.

Many people in the churches who profess that they have an interest in the subject of how to cultivate the

Spirit's companionship are not really willing to give up all to obtain all. They are not willing to turn completely toward God and walk with Him. You may remember that John Bunyan, in his great allegorical writings, often mentioned Mr. Facing Bothways, and we ought to know as well as he did that there are a great many Christians who try to accomplish the difficult task of facing in both directions at the same time. They do want Christ, but they also want some of the world. They allow the Lord to disturb their way, but they also disturb the Lord's way. There is no use talking about being filled with the Spirit and walking in the Spirit, unless we are willing to give up all to obtain all!

Now, this old question in the text, "Can two walk together, except they be agreed?" is a rhetorical question, equivalent to a positive declaration that two cannot walk together except they be agreed, and the affirmation that if the two walk together, they must in some sense be one.

These two, in order to walk together, must agree that they want to walk together, and they must agree that it is to their advantage to have this companionship together. I think you will see that it all adds up to this: For two to walk together voluntarily, they must in some sense be one. They must be unified on the important issues of their walk and companionship and direction if they are going to be committed to traveling together.

I have discovered that some people are just not ready for this teaching of commitment and consecration and devotion to the highest will of God for their lives. They are still facing both ways.

TYPES OF CHRISTIANS

Let me name some of the types of professing Christians who are not ready to give up all to obtain all.

"Insurance" Christians

There are those who are most interested in Christianity for its "insurance" value.

Believe it or not, they want the care and protection that God gives them now, and they want avoidance of hell in time of death. They want the guarantee of heaven at last. To get these things, they seem willing to support the church, give to missions and show a financial interest in other church projects.

Amazing, but true! Some people keep on supporting the church, and they even abstain from some gross pleasures because they want protection—they are interested in the insurance value of Christianity. They want what it has to offer. They are not interested in modernism and liberal Christianity—there isn't any insurance value there.

Are you happy that Jesus Christ died for you on the cross because it means that you will not be brought into judgment, having passed from death into life?

Are you willing to live reasonably well, giving up some gross pleasures as a premium you are paying for the guarantee that God will bless you while you live and take you home to heaven when you die?

Some Christians do not like to have this proposition stated in this manner, for it sort of lets the truth leak out that sets up another question: If this is the basis for our Christian life, are we any better than some of the non-professing sinners?

Not every sinner is dirty, you know. Not every sinner is a rascal. There are honorable men and good men and honest men—men that will tell the truth even if it hurts. They have no hope of eternal life or of heaven to come. They are not followers of our Lord. I have known fine, ethical, honest men who were not Christians.

Actually, I know a man who is so fine and good that everyone wants to make a Christian out of him. He steadfastly refuses and is positive in his statement, "I am not a Christian." He doesn't claim he is winning his way to heaven—he knows he is lost, but he is so good in his life and his ways and his habits that he puts a lot of Christians to shame.

Social Christians

Then, there are those who are not willing because their concept of religion is social and not spiritual.

This includes the people who have watered down the religion of the New Testament until it has no strength, no life, no vitality in it. They water it down with their easy-going opinions. They are very broad-minded—in fact, they are so broad-minded that they cannot walk on the narrow way.

They are socially minded. This is as far as religion goes with them. I am not prepared to say dogmatically that they are not saved, but I am prepared to say that they are not ready for what I am talking about. There is no argument with the fact that the gospel of Christ is essentially spiritual, and Christian truth working upon human souls by the Holy Spirit makes Christian men and women spiritual.

In a similar sense, there are those who are more influenced by the world than by the New Testament, and they are not ready for the Holy Spirit. Of these people, we have to say that they are influenced far more by Hollywood than they are by Jerusalem. Their spirit and mode of life is more like Hollywood than it is like Jerusalem. If you were to suddenly set them down in the New Jerusalem, they would not feel at home because their mode, the texture of their mind, has been created for them by twentieth century entertainment and not by the things of God!

I am positive that much that passes for the gospel in our day is very little more than a mild case of orthodox religion grafted onto a heart that is sold out to the world in its pleasures and tastes and ambitions.

Now, another group that talks about the Holy Spirit but is not prepared for His companionship are those who would like to be filled with the Spirit just for the thrill of it.

I think it is plain that some people want to be thrilled

so badly that they would pay any price—except that they will not die to themselves, nor to the world, nor to the flesh.

For these, what I am about to say now will have no sympathetic meaning whatsoever. It is this: You have never come over into the region where God can get to you! The kind of teaching I have been giving has disturbed some people. If you have been traveling along thinking you are all right, and a man of God begins to insist there is yet much land to be possessed, you will probably be disturbed. That is the preliminary twinge that comes to the soul who wants to know God. Whenever the Word of God reaches us and convicts us, it disturbs us. But this is normal—for God has to jar us loose, even if it takes a disturbance.

When we speak of conviction by the Spirit, we must differentiate between knowing Christian doctrine intellectually and knowing it sympathetically. Anyone can learn creeds and catechisms and recite Christian doctrines from memory, but it is quite another thing to let the Word of God reach us sympathetically. I am talking about the human heart that goes out sympathetically to the Word of God.

I hope that there are many more people hungry for God than I know. God keeps many of His mysteries and secrets from me, so I have no idea how many persons have been helped by my ministry and my preaching. I do thank God for those I know about—some of those who have told me of their "sympathetic" reception of the Word. From somewhere came the deep longing, a blessed aspiration, a yearning after God that is so real and so wonderful and so pain-filled that they know what I am talking about—sympathetically.

HELP FOR THE SPIRITUALLY HUNGRY

Now, if you are a spiritually hungry person, Christ is more than insurance against hell, and Christianity is more than an opportunity to mingle socially with good people. If God is real to you, and Christ is real, and your heart is longing after God's best, I want to give you these pointers to help you in cultivating the Spirit's holy friendship.

Get to Know Him Deeper and Deeper

First, the Holy Spirit is a living Person, and He can be known in an increasing degree of intimacy. Since He is a personality, He can never be fully known in a single encounter.

One of the great mistakes we make is to imagine that by coming to God in the new birth and receiving the Spirit of adoption we know all we can know about God! Similarly, those of us who believe in being filled with the Holy Spirit after conversion also make a mistake in thinking that we know all there is to know about the Holy Spirit.

Oh, my friend, we are just beginning. God's personality is so infinitely rich and manifold that it will take 1,000 years of close search and intimate communion to know even the outer edges of the glorious nature of God. When we talk about communion with God and fellowship with the Holy Spirit, we are talking about that which begins now but will grow and increase and mature while life lasts.

Actually, I do find Christians these days who seem to have largely wasted their lives. They were converted to Christ but they have never sought to go on to an increasing knowledge of God. There is untold loss and failure because they have accepted the whole level of things around them as being normal and desirable.

The Holy Spirit is a living Person, and we can know Him and fellowship with Him! We can whisper to Him, and out of a favorite verse of the Bible or a loved hymn, we hear His voice whispering back. Walking with the Spirit can become a habit. It is a gracious thing to strive to know the things of God through the Spirit of God in a friendship that passes the place where it has to be kept up by chatter.

Be Engrossed with Jesus Christ

How can we cultivate this holy fellowship? Our second pointer is this: Be engrossed with Jesus Christ.

Do you remember that Jesus, on that last day of the feast, lifted up His voice and cried,

He that believeth on me, as the scripture hath said,
out of his belly shall flow rivers of living water. (But
this spake he of the Spirit, which they that believe on
him should receive: for the Holy Ghost was not yet
given; because that Jesus was not yet glorified. (John
7:38–39)

The pouring out of the Holy Spirit depended upon
and waited upon the glorification of Jesus Christ the
Lord. Then, when Pentecost was fully come and Peter
got up to give his great sermon, he referred back to that
same passage and said, in Acts 2:32–33,

This Jesus hath God raised up, whereof we all are
witnesses. Therefore being by the right hand of
God exalted, and having received of the Father the
promise of the Holy Ghost, he hath shed forth this,
which ye now see and hear.

We must always remember that we will know the
Spirit more intimately as we make more of Jesus Christ
the Lord. As Jesus Himself said, a ministry of the Holy
Spirit would be to take the things of Christ and show
them unto us.

Honor Jesus Christ

This brings a companion thought—honor Christ and
the Holy Spirit will honor you. We walk with the Holy

Spirit when we walk with Christ, for Christ will always be where He is honored. The Holy Spirit will honor the one who honors the Savior, Jesus Christ the Lord. Let's honor Him by giving Him His right title. Let's call Him Lord. Let's believe that He is Lord. Let's call Him Christ. Let's believe that He is Christ. Remember that "God hath made that same Jesus, whom ye have crucified, both Lord and Christ" (2:36b), "and set him at his own right hand . . . and hath put all things under his feet, and gave him to be the head over all things to the church" (Ephesians 1:20, 22).

As we honor Jesus, the Spirit of God becomes glad within us. He ceases to hold back, He communes with us and imparts Himself and the sun comes up and heaven comes near as Jesus Christ becomes our All in all.

To glorify Jesus is the business of the Church, and to glorify Jesus is the work of the Holy Spirit. I can walk with Him when I am doing the same things He is doing and going the same way He is going and traveling at the same speed He is traveling. I must honor Him by obedience, by witness, by fellowship.

Walk in Righteousness

There is another pointer: We must walk in righteousness if we are to know the Holy Spirit in increasing intimacy.

Why should we try to argue with the fact that God cannot possibly have sweet fellowship with those who will not live right and walk right?

We have magnified grace in this grace-conscious age. We have magnified grace out of all proportion to the place God gives to it in the Bible. We do have now, as Jude predicted, "ungodly men, turning the grace of our God into lasciviousness, and denying the only Lord God, and our Lord Jesus Christ" (Jude 4). We are so afraid that we will reflect upon the all-sufficiency of grace that we do not dare tell Christians that they must live right.

Paul wrote his epistles in the Holy Spirit, and he laid down holy, inward ethics, moral rules for the inward Christian. You can read them in Romans, Corinthians, Ephesians, Colossians and Galatians.

Read the Sermon on the Mount and the other teachings of Jesus, and you will see that He does expect His people to be clean and pure and right.

Now, I have heard that a Christian brother has said, "Tozer doesn't distinguish between discipleship and salvation. You can be a Christian without being a disciple."

Just let me ask: Who said that you can be a Christian without being a disciple? I don't think you can be a Christian without being a disciple. The idea that I can come to the Lord and by grace have all of my sins forgiven and have my name written in heaven, and have the Carpenter go to work on a mansion in my Father's house, and at the same time raise hell on my way to heaven is impossible and unscriptural. It cannot be found in the Bible.

We are never saved by our good works, but we are not saved apart from good works. Out of our saving faith in Jesus Christ, there springs immediately goodness and righteousness. Spring is not brought by flowers, but you cannot have spring without flowers. It isn't my righteousness that saves, but the salvation I have received brings righteousness.

I think we must face up to this now—that we must walk in righteousness if we are going on to know the Lord. The man who is not ready to live right is not saved, and he will not be saved, and he will be deceived in that great day.

The grace of God that brings salvation teaches the heart that we should deny ungodliness and worldly lusts and live soberly and righteously and godly in this present world. There you have the three dimensions of life: soberly—that is me; righteously—that is my fellow man; and godly—that is God. We ought not to make the mistake of thinking that we can be spiritual and not be good.

I cannot believe that a man is on the road to heaven when he is habitually performing the kind of deeds that would logically indicate that he ought to be on his way to hell.

How can the two walk together except they be agreed? He is the Holy Spirit, and if I walk an unholy way, how can I be in fellowship with Him?

Guard Your Thoughts

The fifth point to help is this: Make your thoughts a clean sanctuary.

God reveals to us that our thoughts are a part of us. Someone has said that "thoughts are things," and the Spirit is all-seeking and all-hearing and all-loving and pure.

Can you imagine a man with malicious and evil thoughts in his heart having companionship with the loving Holy Spirit?

Can you imagine a man bloated with egotism knowing the Holy Spirit in anything like intimacy?

Can you imagine a man who is a deceiver having blessed fellowship with the Holy Spirit? Never!

My friend, if you are habitually given over to thinking and harboring and savoring dirty thoughts, you are habitually without the communion of the Holy Spirit!

Keep your mind pure. Clean out the sanctuary the way old Hezekiah did. They had dirtied up that sanctuary, so when he had taken over, Hezekiah got all of the priests together. It took them days and days, but they carried out all of the filth and burned it, threw it over the bank and got rid of it, and then went back and sanctified the temple. Then the blessed God came and they had their worship again.

Our thoughts are the decorations inside the sanctuary where we live. If our thoughts are purified by the blood of Christ, we are living in a clean room, no matter if we are wearing overalls covered with grease. Our thoughts largely decide the mood and weather and climate within our beings, and God considers our thoughts as part of us. They should be thoughts of peace, thoughts of pity and mercy and kindness, thoughts of charity, thoughts of God and the Son of God—these are pure things, good things and high things.

Therefore, if we would cultivate the Spirit's acquaintance, we must have the control of our thoughts. Our mind ought not to be a wilderness in which every kind of unclean thought makes its own way.

Again, for the kind of fellowship we are talking about, seek to know Him in His Word.

Remember that the Spirit of God inspired the Word and He will be revealed in the Word. I really have no place in my sympathies for those Christians who neglect the Word or ignore the Word or get revelations apart from the Word. This is the Book of God, after all, and if we know the Book well enough, we will have an answer to every problem in the world.

Every problem that touches us is answered in the Book—stay by the Word! I want to preach the Word, love the Word and make the Word the most important element in my Christian life.

Read it much, read it often, brood over it, think over it, meditate over it—meditate on the Word of God day and night. When you are awake at night, think of a helpful verse. When you get up in the morning, no matter how you feel, think of a verse and make the Word of God the important element in your day. The Holy Spirit wrote the Word, and if you make much of the Word, He will make much of you. It is through the Word that He reveals Himself. Between those covers is a living Book. God wrote it and it is still vital and effective and alive. God is in this Book, the Holy Spirit is in this Book, and if you want to find Him, go into this Book.

Let the old saints be our example. They came to the Word of God and meditated. They laid the Bible on the old-fashioned, handmade chair, got down on the old, scrubbed, board floor and meditated on the Word. As they waited, faith mounted. The Spirit and faith illuminated. They had only a Bible with fine print, narrow margins and poor paper, but they knew their Bible better than some of us do with all of our helps.

Let's practice the art of Bible meditation. But please don't grab that phrase and go out and form a club—we are organized to death already. Just meditate. Let us just be plain, thoughtful Christians. Let us open our Bibles, spread them out on a chair and meditate on the Word of God. It will open itself to us, and the Spirit of God will come and brood over it.

I do challenge you to meditate, quietly, reverently, prayerfully, for a month. Put away questions and answers and the filling in of the blank lines in the portions you haven't been able to understand. Put all of the cheap trash away and take the Bible, get on your knees, and in faith, say, "Father, here I am. Begin to teach me!"

He will surely teach you about Himself and about Jesus and about the Spirit and about life and death and heaven and hell, and about His own presence.

Practice His Presence

Finally, our last pointer is to cultivate the art of recognizing the presence of the Spirit everywhere, all of the time.

The Spirit of the Lord fills the world. The Holy Spirit is here and you will find it is impossible to just walk out and hide from His presence. David tried it, and in the 139th Psalm tells how he found out that he could not get away from God.

"If I ascend up into heaven, thou art there: if I make my bed in hell, behold, thou art there. If I . . . dwell in the uttermost parts of the sea; even there shall thy hand lead me, and thy right hand shall hold me" (139:8–10), David said. "If I say, Surely the darkness shall cover me; even the night shall be light about me" (139:11). He testified that he could not get away from the presence of God.

If you are interested in Him, you will find Him where you are. The Presence is all about you. When you awaken in the morning, in place of burying your head behind *The Tribune,* can't you get in just a few thoughts of God while you eat your grapefruit? Remember, cultivating the Holy Spirit's acquaintance is a job. It is something you do, and yet it is so easy and delightful.

Now, I recommend that you find out what it is that has been hindering you in your Christian experience. You have not made progress. You do not know God as well as you did.

It all depends upon how you must answer certain questions about your daily life and habits—some things you do and others that you are not doing. Do these things help to hide the face of Jesus from you? Do these things take the joy out of your spirit? Do they make the Word of God a little less sweet? Do they make earth more desirable and heaven farther away?

Repentance may be necessary. There may be some necessary cleaning up before the Holy Spirit will come and warm your heart and refresh it and make it fragrant with His presence. This is how we cultivate the Spirit's friendship and companionship.

---•---

CHAPTER 9

The Holy Spirit Makes the Difference!

And, behold, I send the promise of my Father upon you: but tarry ye in the city of Jerusalem, until ye be endued with power from on high.

LUKE 24:49

Here we have a very simple and very plain and very forceful truth—the Holy Spirit makes a difference!

Our Lord told His disciples that they had a world-shaking job before them. The job was to preach the gospel of Christ and His redemption and transformation to every creature.

Yet, having told them to go and preach the good news that men could be saved through faith, He forbade them to go. There must have been a most compelling reason for His instructions to wait.

In order for us to assess the great difference in men to whom the Holy Spirit has come in power, we will look first at these disciples to whom Jesus spoke.

Remember that they were His called and chosen disciples.

The Scriptures plainly tell us who they were, and it tells about the long course of instruction by no less a teacher than the Lord Jesus Christ Himself. In this sense, they had graduated from the greatest Bible school in the world. Jesus Himself had taught them for more than three years.

Notice, too, that they had received and possessed a divine authority.

These disciples had an authority that very few people would dare to try to exercise now. Jesus said to them, "Go everywhere. When you cast out devils, when you heal the sick—take all My authority!" He does not give His authority to persons who have had no spiritual experience, you may be sure of that!

These persons to whom Jesus said, "tarry ye . . . until ye be endued with power," (Luke 24:49) actually knew Jesus Christ in a warm and intimate way. They had been with Him throughout the three years; they had seen Him die on a cross; they had seen Him after He had risen from the dead; they knew Him living, dead and living again! They had shown evidence of being truly converted persons.

I know that some people teach that the disciples were converted when the Spirit came upon them at Pentecost. Frankly, I do not believe that at all. That is a modern twist that people have given doctrine in order to make room for their own cold carnality.

I believe the disciples had shown evidence of being truly converted men, and Christ had declared them to be such. If you doubt that, read from the prayer that Jesus made about these disciples in John 17:7–9:

> Now they have known that all things whatsoever thou hast given me are of thee. For I have given unto them the words which thou gavest me; and they have received them, and have known surely that I came out from thee, and they have believed that thou didst send me. I pray for them. . . .

the world, I kept them in thy name: those that thou gavest me I have kept, and none of them is lost, but the son of perdition. . . .” Then He said, in verse 14, “I have given them thy word; and the world hath hated them, because they are not of the world, even as I am not of the world.” These were the things that Jesus said to His Father about His disciples. That doesn’t sound at all like the Lord talking about a bunch of sinners still needing to be converted.

Let me remind you again that Jesus Christ had outlined a program of world evangelization for the disciples and promised that they would receive the power of the Holy Spirit in order to witness effectively unto the uttermost parts of the earth. He said they were to enter a new era.

God was about to introduce a change of dispensation, but He was not to introduce a change of dispensation apart from a stepped-up and elevated spiritual experience.

God has His dispensations in dealing with men, but He doesn't have calendars so He can just pull off January and put up February and thus shift and change dispensations in that way. His dispensations have to do with people—not with calendars. They have to do with spiritual experience, not a measure of time. When they were to enter a new era, it was not only a changeover from one dispensation to another, but it was to be introduced by the coming down of a new afflatus and enabling from above. A power was to be introduced which had not been available before. It was to enter into them and possess them and was to bring God to them in a new way. The power was actually to be a Person—He was to enter them and dwell within them.

That is the difference between Christianity and all the Oriental cults and religions. All cult religions try to wake up what you already have, and Christianity says, "What you have is not enough—you will need the enduement which is sent from above!" That is the difference. The others say, "Stir up the thing that is in you," and they expect this to be enough.

By way of illustration, if there were four or five lions coming at you, you would never think of saying to a little French poodle, "Wake up the lion in you." That would not work—it would not be enough. They would chew the little fellow up and swallow him, haircut and all, because a French poodle just isn't sufficient for a pack of lions. Some power outside of himself would have to make him bigger and stronger than the lion if he were to conquer.

That is exactly what the Holy Spirit says He does for the Christian believer, but the cult religions still say, "Concentrate and free your mind and release the creative powers that lie within you."

The plain fact is, such creative powers do not lie within us. We begin to die the moment we are born. I have often wondered why babies cry just as soon as they are born—could it be that they don't want to die? They start to die the minute they are born. All of this teaching about hidden potentials and creative impulses and waking up your true self is hard to defend, for we walk around on the earth barely able to keep going. And as we get older, gravitation will pull and slowly drag us down and finally bump over us. We finally give up with a sigh and go back to mother earth. That's the kind of potential that the human race has—the potential to be a corpse.

God Almighty is saying to us, "I am not wanting to wake up the power that lies in you. You shall receive the power of the Holy Spirit coming upon you!" That is a different thing altogether. If we had only to be awakened, the Lord would simply have gone around waking us up—but we need more than this. We need to be endued with power from on high.

So, they were to enter a new era, and it was to be marked by something grandly new—an enriched spiritual condition. What, then, are the differences that we see in these disciples as a result?

First, in order to clear the ground, we will take a look at some of the things that these disciples possessed before the Holy Spirit came, and therefore, obviously, there were blessings that He did not have to bring at Pentecost.

For instance, they were true disciples, and they possessed the consciousness of their discipleship and their authority from Christ. They were the Lord's own loving disciples. That did not come at Pentecost. They were converted, forgiven and had fellowship with Christ, and they had something a lot of ministers do not have now—they had the gift of preaching: "They . . . went through the towns, preaching the gospel, and healing every where" (Luke 9:6)!

Again, they had the power to work miracles, so that when they came back reciting the manifestations of their power, the Lord rebuked them for pride and told them they should be glad, rather, that their names were written in heaven. But He did not deny that they had exercised His power, for He knew they did. He gave it to them! Some teach that if you are filled with the Spirit, you will have miracles, forgetting that the disciples had the power of miracles before they were filled with the Spirit.

The power of the Holy Spirit is not necessary to make miracle workers. The power of the Holy Spirit is something infinitely higher, grander and more wonderful than that. They worked miracles before the Spirit ever came.

Now, consider the difference in their lives and experiences when the Holy Spirit came upon them, when they were no longer in the pre-Pentecost days, but when they were in the post-Pentecost era after the outpouring of the Holy Spirit.

WHAT THE HOLY SPIRIT DID FOR THEM

It is easy to list seven things that the Holy Spirit did for them, and you can check each one with the Scriptures. I think we ought to put the emphasis where God puts it, continue to put it there, expounding the Scriptures and staying by the plain teaching of the Scriptures. Now here they are:

They Knew His Presence

First, they knew the sudden, brilliant consciousness of the actual presence of the living God.

They knew Jesus and they loved Him, but in the coming of the Holy Spirit there was the sudden, illuminating knowledge of God Himself actually being present with them. A veil was torn away, and they felt God, and the sense of acute God-consciousness was on them from that moment. They knew themselves to be in immediate contact with another world, and that is exactly what the average gospel church does not have today.

We are not in contact with another world—in fact, we

are very happily in contact with this world and what it can offer. Those disciples were "otherworldly." I believe that a sense of God and heaven ought to be upon us. We ought to live with a knowledge and consciousness of God and heaven on us day by day, whether we are businessmen, farmers, schoolteachers, housewives, students or whatever we are.

I can tell you that only the Holy Spirit can give and bring and impart and maintain that sense of the Divine presence. For those disciples at Pentecost, it was as if a cloud had been rolled back and a city of God, before unsuspected and unseen, now suddenly became clearly visible before their eyes.

They Received Joy

The second difference was this: They actually received the joy of the Holy Spirit.

We can note the change of the emotional tone which came at once. In the four Gospels, there was not too much joy. There was instruction, and there was a subdued and quiet peace, but not very much joy. When they got over into the book of Acts, they changed from the minor key into the major. This makes me think of the old Jewish songs written in a minor key. They are sad and gloomy, without true joy. They groan and moan and plead and lament, but they never arrive at the answer of inward joy.

I am thinking about God's dear people always praying for joy, praying for light, praying for every benediction, and yet they don't receive. They work themselves up on Sunday, then go back down and start on a lower level on Monday. Perhaps they work themselves up a little by Wednesday evening, but it never seems to stick. The bell loses its tongue, its clapper. It doesn't ring anymore.

Well, the joy and happiness of these disciples was now the joy and blessing and delight of the Holy Spirit. Their happiness was no longer the happiness of Adam—it was not the happiness of nature. Human beings are busy trying to work up a joy of some sort. They try it in dance halls, they try it with rock and roll bands, they turn to television programs. But we still don't see the truly happy faces—people always seem to be in a cold trance of some sort. That is the effort to work Adam up into joy, and Adam is not basically happy. Adam has to die and go back to earth again and go to hell, unless he is converted through the blood of Christ.

No, the human race is not basically happy—we are anything else but! The joy of the Holy Spirit is not something worked up; it is a post-resurrection joy. Christ came out of the grave, and the Spirit of the risen Christ comes back to His people. The joy that we have is the joy that looks back on the grave. This is not a joy that we have in spite of the knowledge that we must die; it is a joy that results from the fact that in Christ we have already died, and risen, and there is no real death out there for the true child of God.

They Preached with Power

The third difference which the Holy Spirit made was the striking power of their words to penetrate and arrest.

I don't have to tell you that there is a difference in the penetrating power of words. The same words, the same sentence spoken by one man will put you under conviction, but spoken by another man can leave you completely cold. That is the difference made by the Holy Spirit. Jesus said, "ye shall receive power" (Acts 1:8), and the word "power" means the ability to do. When Peter preached at Pentecost, they were stricken in their hearts when they heard him. They were pierced. In Acts 2, it says, "Now when they heard this, they were pricked in their heart, and said unto Peter and to the rest of the apostles, Men and brethren, what shall we do?" (2:37). That is the pricking in the heart.

I don't quote Greek very often because it gives the impression that a man knows more than he does. But when it says in the Gospel of John that the soldier pierced the side of Jesus (John 19:34), the Greek word used is not as strong as the word "pricked," which is used here in Acts. To sum up, the words of Peter at Pentecost went further into the hearts of the hearers than the spear went into the body of Jesus. The word is stronger in the Greek. The Holy Spirit penetrated, and that is one of the works of the Holy Spirit. He comes and He penetrates. He sharpens the point of the arrows of the man of God. Moody said that he preached the same sermons after he was filled with the Spirit, but found a mighty difference—because he then possessed that power that penetrated. Before, he simply tried to reason with people, begging them and coaxing them to come. Afterward, there was the divine penetration that went straight through—beyond their reasoning power into their being.

They Had Authority

In the fourth place, there was suddenly the clear sense of the reality of all things.

You will notice that throughout the four Gospels the disciples were asking questions—while in the book of Acts and after Pentecost they were answering questions. That is the difference between the man who is Spirit-filled and the man who is not. The preacher who is not filled with the Spirit uses many phrases like, "And now, let us ask ourselves this question." I know you have heard that from the pulpit—"Now let us ask ourselves. . . ." I have often wondered why the reverend wanted to ask himself a question. Why didn't he settle that in his study before he came into the pulpit? "What shall we say?" and "What should we think?" God never puts a preacher in the pulpit to ask questions. He puts the preacher in the pulpit to answer questions. He puts him there with authority to stand up in the name of God and speak and answer questions.

In the four Gospels, the disciples had asked many questions. "Lord, shall it be? Lord, how shall it be? Lord, who? Lord, what?" But now they stood with authority and answered questions. The same Peter who had sneaked around and warmed his hands at the world's fire and lied to the little woman who recognized his accent (Matthew 26:69–74) was standing boldly to preach the Word of the Lord. There was a difference. There was authority.

I don't want to be unkind, but I am sure there ought to be a lot more authority in the pulpit than there is now. A preacher should reign from his pulpit as a king from his throne. He should not reign by law nor by regulations and not by board meetings or man's authority. He ought to reign by moral ascendancy.

When a man of God stands to speak, he ought to have the authority of God on him so that he makes the people responsible to listen to him. When they will not listen to him, they are accountable to God for turning away from the divine Word. In place of that needed authority, we have tabby cats with their claws carefully trimmed in the seminary, so they can paw over the congregations and never scratch them at all. They have had their claws trimmed and are just as soft and sweet as can be.

Let me tell you that I was converted from hearing a fellow who preached on the street corner. I was a young working man, and I joined the nearest church—I didn't know any better. The first time I shook hands with the pastor was like shaking hands with a baby—he had not done a lick of work since he was eighteen, I am sure, because his hands were so soft. I remember he preached one Sunday about a harp, using the subject, "A Harp of a Thousand Strings." He didn't say much, but he said it beautifully, and it ended up like this, "So I am sure that the soul of a man is the harp of a thousand strings."

I went home—and didn't hear any harp. I didn't hear any authority. I believe in the authority of God, and I believe if a man doesn't have it, he should go away and pray and wait until he gets the authority and then stand up to speak even if he has to begin by preaching on a soapbox on a street corner. Go to a rescue mission and preach with authority! They had it in those days—when they stood up, there was authority!

They Were Separated

The fifth thing was this: The filling of the Holy Spirit brings a sharp separation between the believer and the world.

Actually, after Pentecost, they were looking at another world. They really saw another world.

Nowadays, we perceive that even a large part of evangelical Christianity is trying to convert this world to the Church. We are bringing the world in head over heels—unregenerate, uncleansed, unshriven, unbaptized, unsanctified. We are bringing the world right into the Church. If we can just get some big shot to say something nice about the Church, we rush into print and tell about this fellow and what nice things he said. I don't care at all about big shots, because I serve a living Savior, and Jesus Christ is Lord of lords and King of kings. I believe every man ought to know this ability to see another world.

They Became Men of Prayer

The sixth great difference was this: They took a great delight in prayer and communion with God. Do you recall that in the times of prayer recorded in the Gospels the only one who could stay awake was Jesus? Others tried to pray, but they came to Him and said, "Teach us to pray" (Luke 11:1). He knew that you cannot just teach someone to pray. Some of the churches now advertise courses on how to pray. How ridiculous! That is like giving a course on how to fall in love. When the Holy Spirit comes He takes the things of God and translates them into language our hearts can understand. Even if we do not know the will of God, the Holy Spirit does know, and He prays "with groanings which cannot be uttered" (Romans 8:26). These disciples were praying people—in the book of Acts you will find them in prayer meetings. But before that, they would fall asleep. The difference was by the Spirit—now they had great delight in prayer.

They Loved the Scriptures

The seventh and final thought concerns the manner in which they loved the Scriptures of God.

You will notice that Jesus quoted the Scriptures in the Gospels, but the disciples quoted the Scriptures in the book of Acts. There was a difference! I remember hearing a dear saint of God say, "When I was filled with the

Spirit, I loved the Scriptures so much that if I could have gotten more of the Word of God inside of me by eating it, I would have eaten the Book. I literally would have taken and eaten it—leather and everything—if I could have gotten more of the Book inside my heart."

Well, you don't get it by eating it, but the Word of God is sweet to the Spirit-filled person because the Spirit wrote the Scriptures. You cannot read the Scriptures with a spirit of Adam, for they were inspired by the Spirit of God. The spirit of the world does not appreciate the Scriptures—it is the Spirit of God who gives appreciation of the Scriptures. One little flash of the Holy Spirit will give you more inward, divine illumination on the meaning of the text than all the commentators that ever commented. Yes, I have commentaries—I am just trying to show you that if you have everything else and have not the fullness of the Spirit, you have nothing. When you do have the Holy Spirit, then God can use anything and everything to aid in our illumination.

In our day, we are prone to live by hearsay. Our sense of reality has been blurred, and it has become vague. The "wonder" has all gone out of it.

It is just here that I should relate the things that happened in Europe among the Moravians in 1727. They were quiet people, like you and me, but they waited and prepared their hearts, and one morning, suddenly, that which they called "a sense of the living nearness of the Savior, instantaneously bestowed," came upon them.

Now, when the Holy Spirit is allowed to come with particular intimacy in a human soul, He never talks about Himself, but always about the Lord Jesus Christ.

He comes to reveal Jesus, and although it was the Holy Spirit who fell on that Moravian company in 1727, they did not speak of a sense of the loving nearness of the Spirit. They said, "a sense of the loving nearness of the Savior, instantaneously bestowed."

Count Zinzendorf wrote that the small group of seventy-five German Christians arose and went out from that building so happy and joyful that they did not know whether they were on earth or had gone on to heaven. The historian says that, as a result of that experience, within twenty short years those Spirit-filled Moravian Christians did more for world missions than the entire Church in all of its parts had done in 200 years. It made missionaries of them, and they bathed their work and their mission in prayer.

Do you know what happened? The Moravians got a man converted—Charles Wesley, and then his brother, John Wesley. John was crossing the Atlantic Ocean and such a storm came up that even the sailors were scared. John Wesley found that only a little group of Moravian Christians were not afraid. They huddled together and sang hymns with shining faces. Asked why they did not pray and why they were happy, they answered, "If the Lord wills to have us all drown, sudden death will be sudden glory!"

Wesley, the dignified Anglican, did not know what to make of that, but the answer went deep into his own soul. He went to talk to his brother, Charles, and found that he had already been converted.

Then John went to Peter Bowler, the Moravian, and said, "Peter, my brother Peter, I do not have what you have, and I don't have what my brother Charles has. What will I do?"

Bowler answered, "It is by grace, brother, it is all by grace!"

John Wesley said, "Well, I don't have grace. What will I do? Should I quit preaching?"

Peter Bowler said to him, "Preach grace because it is in the Bible, and then after you get it, preach it because you have it!"

Soon John Wesley felt his heart strangely warmed, and later Methodism spread all throughout the world. The Salvation Army was born out of that same Pentecostal outpouring among the Moravians in 1727. There was nothing radical, there were no tongues, no one climbed a tent pole or crawled in the straw. These were good, well-behaved Germans, but the Holy Spirit came where He ought to be—within them, making Jesus real. They were so filled with joy that they could hardly stay alive.

The New Testament speaks of the sense of "wonder" among the early Christians. The Church in our day seems to have lost this. We can explain everything, but there is a constant note of joyous surprise running through the book of Acts and over into the epistles. Daily, they were enjoying the blessed surprises of the living God. He blessed them to a point of amazement.

I remember that Dr. R. R. Brown, of Omaha, once said to me, "God is so good to me that it frightens me!" He used the word frighten rather than amaze, but that's what I mean. The quality of wonder lies upon us since the Holy Spirit has come, and this is what we need. May God grant it! Without any doubt, the Holy Spirit makes the difference!

———————————•———————————

CHAPTER 10

The Heavenly Dove: Repelled by Corruption

*And God saw that the wickedness of man was great in the
earth, and that every imagination of the thoughts of his heart
was only evil continually. And it repented the LORD that he had
made man on the earth, and it grieved him at his heart. And
the LORD said, I will destroy man whom I have created from the
face of the earth; both man, and beast, and the creeping thing,
and the fowls of the air; for it repenteth
me that I have made them.*

GENESIS 6:5–7

*And God said unto Noah, The end of all flesh is come before
me; for the earth is filled with violence through them; and,
behold, I will destroy them with the earth. Make thee an ark
of gopher wood; rooms shalt thou make in the ark, and shalt
pitch it within and without with pitch.*

6:13–14

*In the six hundredth year of Noah's life, in the second month,
the seventeenth day of the month, the same day were all the
fountains of the great deep broken up, and the windows of*

heaven were opened. And the rain was upon the earth forty days and forty nights.

7:11–12

And all flesh died that moved upon the earth, both of fowl, and of cattle, and of beast, and of every creeping thing that creepeth upon the earth, and every man.... And every living substance was destroyed which was upon the face of the ground, both man, and cattle, and the creeping things, and the fowl of the heaven; and they were destroyed from the earth: and Noah only remained alive, and they that were with him in the ark.

7:21, 23

And it came to pass at the end of forty days, that Noah opened the window of the ark which he had made: and he sent forth a raven, which went forth to and fro, until the waters were dried up from off the earth. Also he sent forth a dove from him, to see if the waters were abated from off the face of the ground; but the dove found no rest for the sole of her foot, and she returned unto him into the ark, for the waters were on the face of the whole earth: then he put forth his hand, and took her, and pulled her in unto him into the ark. And he stayed yet other seven days; and again he sent forth the dove out of the ark; and the dove came in to him in the evening; and, lo, in her mouth was an olive leaf pluckt off: so Noah knew that the waters were abated from off the earth. And he stayed yet other seven days; and sent forth the dove; which returned not again unto him any more.

8:6–12

We are going to pay particular attention to Genesis 8:9, "But the dove found no rest for the sole of her foot...."

First, however, we must think about the kind of world which God saw and judged before the flood.

God searched into the hearts of men and He saw that mankind was corrupt and wicked, filled with evil thoughts and imaginations continually. And what does He see now? This is a good place to be reminded of what the Word of God says about the need of the Holy Spirit in our world, and the true evaluation of those whom the world calls its "good men."

THE WORLD VS. THE SPIRIT

Why did Jesus say, when He spoke of the Holy Spirit, "the world cannot receive, because it seeth him not, neither knoweth him" (John 14:17)? There is one thing that Christians ought to get in their minds—the fact that the world knows nothing about the Holy Spirit. The world knows nothing about the Spirit, but the world talks about its good men. The world appreciates a good man if he gives to colleges and hospitals. Books are written about him and he becomes a celebrity if he runs a clinic to take care of the lepers. The world knows about good men, but the world has absolutely no affinity for the Holy Spirit, because even good men are under the judgment of God. The best that we have in the world, our universities, our humanitarian societies, the best we have apart from the new birth, apart from the presence of God in the life of a man, is only corruption, and the wrath of God is upon it. The world cannot receive the Spirit of God!

The result of what God saw among men was grief to God's own heart—and only love can grieve. You cannot grieve unless you love. God loved the man whom He had made and the degenerate and corrupt race that had descended from Him. God's love caused Him to grieve, and it filled Him with anxious care.

JUDGMENT AND MERCY

Sometimes the kindest thing the physician can do is to call for amputation—otherwise, the patient will die. God, who loved mankind, looked upon man and saw that moral corruption had gone out into all the bloodstream and was in all the tissues and cells. He knew that the patient would die unless He sent kindly judgment to destroy it. He would save the few to start over, that the race might not perish borne down by the weight of its own sin. God sent a judgment on the earth, and the waters covered the earth, as they had formerly covered the sea.

After the passing of a great number of days, the ark still floated with the eight persons aboard, the animals, the birds and all the other creatures. Outside the ark, the water had long passed the flood stage where people and things were simply dead. Corruption had already started to set in.

Noah opened the ark when it settled on Mount Ararat. You see, the windows of the ark were upward toward heaven, and there apparently were no portals so Noah could look down. Noah decided to find out from the bird if there was dry ground below. He wanted to know if the waters of judgment had abated. He opened the window and pushed the raven out.

Here we have a sight which is probably hard to visualize or understand. We see a dark bird sailing across the desolation. Now what was that desolation? What did it amount to? What did it add up to? It added up to the judgment of God. The angry displeasure of God was on the world. The waters of judgment, the boiling silt, the floating corpses, all of the dead things and lots of flotsam and jetsam over the waters are the marks of the judgment of God upon the world. The dark bird sailed across the desolation, and his dark heart felt at home there, for he was a carrion eater, and he felt at home among the carrion. As the raven sailed away from the warm, lighted ark and from the presence of Noah, he croaked with delight.

The evidence of death and judgment should have been a repulsive and horrible sight, but the raven was built for it. Something in his dark heart loved it, because he lived on it. He immediately sailed down and lighted on a near and likely corpse. He began to tear hunks of half-rotten flesh with his strong claws and beak. He tore away and ate until he was stuffed and sleepy with overeating. Then, fastening his claws down into the floating thing, happy and restful, he went to sleep croaking a goodnight word. The happiness that he had found was what his heart wanted. Corruption and desolation, silt and dirt, rotten flesh and dead things—all fitted his disposition and his temperament. He fed on the floating dead.

Mankind Like the Raven

This is a brilliant illustration of how things are in the world today. When man sinned, and God deserted him and he deserted God, he went out from the place that had been Eden and began to propagate himself, even though he had the judgment of God upon him. "For in the day that thou eatest thereof thou shalt surely die" (Genesis 2:17). "And as it is appointed unto men once to die, but after this the judgment" (Hebrews 9:27), God promised.

God says that He is displeased with every man, and unless we repent, we shall all perish. All the nations of the world shall be turned into hell. God is displeased with the nations of the world. He is displeased with the East, and He is displeased with the West. He will send His judgment on oppressive governments, and He will send His judgment on the so-called free nations of the world as well. The great judgment of God is upon mankind, all the stock of mankind—red, yellow, black, white, educated and uneducated, cultured and uncultured, cave men and learned men around the world. Yet it does not seem to bother people because man has in him that thing we call sin. It does not bother him at all, because he is just as the raven was—at home in the desolation. His dark heart had an affinity for judgment and desolation. Man also finds himself at home in a world under the judgment of God.

There was only one good Man that ever came to the world. He managed to stay alive just thirty-three years—then they took Him out and nailed Him on the cross. The better a man is, the more he is despised by those who love the desolation, the darkness and the sin of the world. Just as the raven didn't come back to the ark, but lived out there in the desolation, so men have built their civilization upon floating death. We would like to think otherwise. We are proud of our culture. We are proud of our bridges, our roads, our space progress, our education and all the things that we can do. God looks on the heart and says, "The world is filled with violence." It is filled with violence and it is filled with corruption now.

No Place for the Dove to Land

I think that the most terrifying thing that the sensitive Christian heart can hear is the whirring of the wings of God. God wants to come down. He wants to get into our houses of Parliament, our Congress and Senate. He wants to get into our United Nations. He wants to get into our groups that play baseball and hockey. God wants to get in, but He can't get in because the judgment—His wrath—is upon men. His fury is upon a corrupt, violent and vicious world. The Holy Spirit is restless and He can't come down. He would come down, for He loves mankind. He loves the blackest sinner in all the world and that might be you or me. Sin is of the heart as well as of the body and of conduct.

I suppose I would not speak about all this if all I had to say was that the world could not receive the Holy Spirit. That which gives me the most concern is that the Holy Spirit cannot even light upon Christians. Now, every Christian has a measure of the Holy Spirit. Let's get that straight. "Now if any man have not the Spirit of Christ, he is none of his" (Romans 8:9). When the Holy Spirit convicts a man and regenerates a man, there's a deposit of the Holy Spirit in the life of that man.

The Holy Spirit is in some measure resident in the breast of everyone that is converted. Otherwise, there wouldn't be conversion. The Holy Spirit doesn't stand outside a man and regenerate him; He comes in to regenerate him. That is one thing and we're glad and grateful for that, but it's quite another thing for the Holy Spirit to come down with His wings outspread, uninhibited, free and pleased to fill lives, and to fill churches, and to fill denominations. That's quite another thing.

That some measure of the Spirit is in the breast of every converted man is good and right and real. It is also true that the Holy Spirit wants to come down, as the dove wanted to land on the dry ground and could find no place for the sole of her foot. In our day, too, the Spirit seeks a resting place for His feet, and we have called these visitations "revivals"—and we're languishing for the lighting down of the Spirit!

I have to tell the truth, and the truth is not very well received, even by the saints. The simple truth is that unless we have a lighting down upon evangelicalism, upon fundamentalism, upon our gospel churches, unless the Dove of God can come down with His wings outspread and make Himself known and felt among us, that which is fundamentalism will be liberalism in years to come. And liberalism will be unitarianism.

JUDGMENT IS COMING

This world is not a friend to grace to lead us on to God. We are going in the other direction. Have you thought about it, or are you simply running around being entertained? Have you thought about all this? You and I have to face judgment one of these days. You and I are going to stand before the Man whose eyes are like fire, and out of whose mouth there comes a sharp, two-edged sword, and we are going to have to talk to Him about deeds done in the body, and we're going to have to face what Wesley called "The Great Assize" and there be judged for the deeds done in the body. This is not the Great White Throne judgment, which is for sinners, but another judgment which is for Christians. We're going to have to show Him that we've been serious about all this. We weren't out to be entertained, we were out to be holy!

The Spirit is seeking a rest for the sole of His foot. He

is seeking it, and I hear the fluttering of holy wings, and I hear the mourning sound of Him who is grieved and quenched. I see Him looking about for signs of repentance, for signs of sorrow of heart and the lifting of the judgment of God from the Church. When God judges the world, it will be terror and fire, but God wants to judge the Church. He wants to judge you and me—His children. He wants to begin at the house of the Lord, and He wants to begin to judge us, and the absence of the full power of the Holy Spirit is perpetual condemnation.

Now, what are the marks of God's displeasure upon His people? Well, let me name a few of them for you. There are sins of act and habit, sins of selfishness, such as reveling in wealth while the world starves, living like kings while millions perish—and sins of the heart such as lust.

You know, you can be a Christian, or at least you can belong to a good church and still have lust in your heart. You can belong to a good church and still have spite in your heart. You go before the pastor or the elders or deacons or whoever takes them into your church, and they cannot look in your heart to find out whether you have lust in there. We have all cultivated the religious smile, and we manage to look pious when the occasion comes. When we apply for membership, we smile piously, and they say that he's a fine young man—but in his heart there is lust.

God hates it, and the Dove won't come down!

We can't look into a woman's heart and see that she is

spiteful because the woman across the street has a longer car than she has, or a more expensive fur coat. There are churches where deacons and elders sit on the same board for years with unconfessed resentment in their hearts.

Resentment in the heart of a man is just as bad as adultery. Resentment or spite in the heart of a woman is just as bad as the world.

The man of the world is doing the only thing he knows to do, and I wonder if he is any worse than the so-called pious people who have spite, resentment or jealousy in the heart.

I've met people that lived year after year with resentment, but I just will not stay mad at anybody. I absolutely refuse. I come from a fiery, nervous English strain. My father had a temper like the trigger on an atom bomb, and he could blow up. I have seen him take a shovel and beat a wheelbarrow in anger—just beat a wheelbarrow. But I won't stay sour at anybody. I refuse to have resentment and ill will and an unforgiving spirit eating at my vitals. Forgive the fellow, and you'll feel better inside! Yet we have spite, we have jealousy, we have envy and we have pride— pride of person, pride of creed, pride of possession, pride of race and pride of accomplishment.

We also have coldness of heart toward the Godhead. We sing about God and we pray, but it lacks warmth. We worship coldly and stiffly. God must have looked toward the languishing Church back in Israel, when the man of God warned the Jews and said, "Woe to them that are at ease in Zion . . . That lie upon beds of ivory . . . That chant to the sound of the viol, and invent to themselves instruments of musick, like David . . . but they are not grieved for the affliction of Joseph" (Amos 6:1, 4–6). We are fundamentalists, sure we are! We carry our Scofield Bibles, sure we do! We are evangelicals, but the Church is languishing, and we don't care—at least we don't care very much!

NO CONCERN FOR THE LOST

Then there's the poor sick world out there. I, for my part, do not want to be happy while the world perishes. Nobody loves the world quite enough. The Man who loved the world enough to die for it died for it, and Paul, the man who loved Israel enough to want to perish for Israel, cried out he wanted to be accursed for Israel's sake. We don't seem to have it much these days. Much of our Christianity is social instead of spiritual. We should be a spiritual body with social overtones, but most of our churches are social bodies with spiritual overtones. The heart of the Church ought always to be Christ and the Holy Spirit. The heart of the Church ought always to be heaven and God and righteousness. Those who loved the Lord spoke often one to another, and what they spoke about were spiritual things.

I have met men who wouldn't talk to you about anything but God. There was a Canadian named Robert Jaffray, whose family published the Toronto *Globe and Mail*. He became a Christian and pulled away from his family over their protest and went to the mission field. That man of God, that good, godly man spent years searching for the lost and winning them! He was always reading maps and going where no man in his condition should ever have gone. He was overweight, had diabetes, and it was difficult for him to eat right. Yet he went on and on and on, and lived on whatever he could find to eat. He lived among the poor and miserable peoples of the world, always saying to God, "Let my people go!" (Exodus 5:1). Robert Jaffray got to the place where you couldn't talk to him and just discuss common things. You couldn't do it—he would look down and answer and then begin to talk about God and missions. I have met saints like that—people who were so interested in the things of God that nothing else mattered. My brother and sister, the Holy Spirit loves people like that. He loves that kind of spirit, and He is quick to come, to fill, to take over and to take charge. Now God is looking for a people who want to be right. He is looking for a little spot where the waters of His displeasure are dried up, where there is no more judgment, no more death, where the silt and filth are all cleaned away and where the blessed Holy Spirit can come down in power. He wants to do that beginning with us and for all of us!

A Story of a Tender Heart

Let me share a true story with you. I was traveling on the train at one time, when a man I knew got on and sat down beside me. He was a missionary, and he seemed very tender and broken.

He said, "I'd like to ask you something, Mr. Tozer. I am troubled, and this is my problem. A number of years ago, a strange thing happened on our mission compound in India. We had been having blessing and everything was going all right. The missionaries got together for a conference, and the native Christians were there, as well. We were all sitting around together, and a Presbyterian missionary was asked to preach to us. He preached and he sat down.

"Mr. Tozer, I will never be able to describe what happened, and I don't know why it happened, but suddenly there came down on that assembly something like a wave of love and light that broke us up completely.

"One missionary ran to another and said, 'Forgive me, forgive me,' and another ran to another, and they wept and hugged each other. As a result of this experience, my home has been completely transformed. Now, my wife and I were getting on perfectly well, a normal Christian home, but, oh, the difference since that time! Home is heaven now.

"But this is what bothers me. Since that time, I'm so tender, and I weep so easily that it bothers me. When I get up to preach, I am just as likely as not to break down and cry. I never was that way before, but since the coming down that day, the sudden, wonderful visitation in India, I just cry so easily.

"Coming home on the ship, I had this experience. They asked me to take chapel on ship one morning. They told me there were some communists who would be present in the service. I took my text and there it came again, the memory of all the glory came down on me, and I just began to cry and couldn't finish my sermon."

I said, "What did the communists think of it? Did they make fun of you?"

"Oh, no," he said. "They were very reverent about it. I'm not saying anything good about a communist—I can't—but at least in this case the Holy Spirit had shut the mouths of the communists."

Then I said to my friend, "You have asked me for advice on how you can overcome your tender heart. Brother, don't try it! We have too many dry preachers in the world now. We have so many dry preachers and so many men who never shed a tear. If you can keep the tears of God on you and can keep your heart tender, brother, keep it! You have a treasure you should never give up."

Do you know how he got that way? The coming down, the lighting down—and they got right with one another. They got cleaned up—they got trouble out of their hearts, and they got sins put away. Even missionaries got their sins put away, and when there was no more evidence of the displeasure of the Almighty God, the Holy Spirit came down!

TITLES BY A.W. TOZER

More from A. W. Tozer:

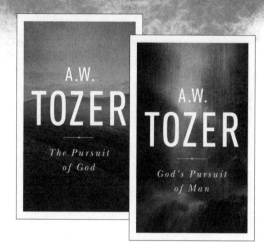

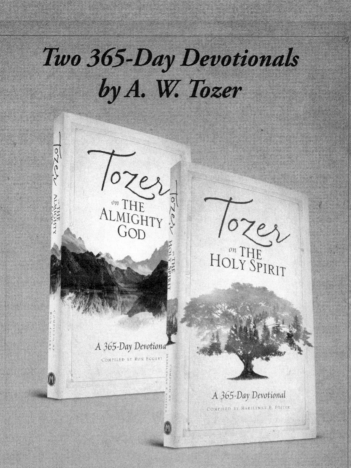

*From the Word **to Life***

Moody Radio produces and delivers compelling programs filled with biblical insights and creative expressions of faith that help you take the next step in your relationship with Christ.

You can hear Moody Radio on 36 stations and more than 1,500 radio outlets across the U.S. and Canada. Or listen on your smartphone with the Moody Radio app!

www.moodyradio.org